Menno Simons' Life and Writings

A Quadricentennial Tribute
1536–1936

BIOGRAPHY
by
HAROLD S. BENDER

WRITINGS
Selected and Translated from the Dutch by
JOHN HORSCH

Wipf and Stock Publishers
EUGENE, OREGON

Wipf and Stock Publishers
199 West 8th Avenue, Suite 3
Eugene, Oregon 97401

Menno Simons' Life and Writings
A Quadricentennial Tribute 1536-1936
By Bender, Harold S.
Copyright© January, 1936 Herald Press
ISBN: 1-59244-259-5
Publication date: June, 2003 .
Previously published by Herald Press, January, 1936 .

Printed in the United States of America

PREFACE

The year of the four hundredth anniversary of Menno Simons' renunciation of Catholicism finds us with no available biography of Menno in English. J. Newton Brown's very brief and inadequate sketch, *The Life and Times of Menno, the Celebrated Dutch Reformer,* published at Philadelphia in 1853, has long since been forgotten, and the modern biography by John Horsch, *Menno Simons, His Life, Labors, and Teachings,* published at Scottdale, Pennsylvania in 1916, which has served us well for twenty years, has just gone out of print. In this anniversary year when the commemoration of Menno Simons' conversion revives our appreciation of the service which he rendered to the cause of evangelical Christianity and the cause of the Mennonite Church in particular, it is desirable that a comprehensive, popular account of his life and work be made widely available. This is particularly true in a year and at a time in world affairs when, in the midst of economic confusion and distress and fearful rumors of war, the voice of Menno Simons can profitably be heard with its calm but convinced insistence upon a thoroughgoing practical Christianity making the whole of life subject to the lordship of Christ, and with its demand that men resolutely abandon all carnal strife and live together in peace and love.

In preparing a popular biography of Menno Simons which might be read with pleasure and profit by both old and young, it seemed good to avoid both the style and the forms and thereby possibly the impediments of learning, without sacrificing scrupulous accuracy in detail. What is

▼

PREFACE

here presented is in essence based upon the work by John Horsch named above and the most recent biography of Menno Simons submitted as a doctoral dissertation at the University of Heidelberg, Germany, in February, 1936 by Dr. Cornelius Krahn. I am greatly indebted to these two good friends, to Dr. Krahn for the privilege of reading his manuscript before its publication, and to John Horsch for his careful reading of the manuscript and his many valuable suggestions.

The English edition of Menno's complete works, which was published as a large quarto volume at Elkhart, Indiana, in 1876-1881, will soon disappear from the market, and it is to be hoped that before many years have passed a new edition of the complete works in an up-to-date translation will be available. But many who will not read the complete works in either the old or the new edition will no doubt be glad for a more convenient collection of the best of Menno's thought. To meet this demand, selections from Menno's most significant writings have been added to the biography. These selections have been made by John Horsch, who has also made the translations into the English from the original Dutch; they constitute for the most part a revision of a similar collection of extracts which appeared in his 1916 work on Menno Simons.

HAROLD S. BENDER.

Goshen, Indiana
June 1, 1936

CONTENTS

Chapter		Page
	Preface	v
I	The Catholic Priest	1
II	Conversion and Renunciation of Catholicism 1535-1536	15
III	Labors in Holland 1536-1543	25
IV	Labors in Northwest Germany 1543-1546	30
V	Labors in Holstein 1546-1561	35
VI	The Significance of Menno Simons	51
	Writings	55-110

1. The Authority of the Scriptures 55
2. The Trinity of God 56
3. Christ, His Deity and Humanity 57
4. The Incarnation 59
5. The Holy Spirit 60
6. Sin 61
7. The Atonement 62
8. Repentance 64
9. Faith 65
10. Justification by Faith 67
11. Regeneration 68
12. Holiness of Life 70
13. The Church 72
14. Called out from the World 74
15. A True Brotherhood 75
16. The Ordinances 77
17. Baptism 78
18. Import of Baptism 80
19. Infant Baptism 81
20. Salvation of Infants 83
21. The Error of Baptismal Regeneration 84
22. The Lord's Supper 85
23. Discipline 86

CONTENTS

		Page
24.	Repentance in Case of Secret Sin...............	87
25.	The Missionary Calling of the Church...........	88
26.	Nonresistance..................................	89
27.	Swearing of Oaths..............................	92
28.	Capital Punishment.............................	93
29.	Nonconformity to the World.....................	94
30.	Liberty of Conscience..........................	95
31.	Predestination.................................	98
32.	Perfectionism..................................	99
33.	New Revelations................................	100
34.	Higher Education...............................	100
35.	Anti-Secrecy...................................	101
36.	Attitude Toward Other Denominations............	101
37.	Examples of Consecration to the Lord's Service.	102
38.	Laboring under Difficulties....................	104
39.	Persecution....................................	106
40.	A Prayer of Menno Simons.......................	109

MAP.. 48
CHRONOLOGICAL LIST OF MENNO SIMONS' WRITINGS.... 111

CHAPTER I

THE CATHOLIC PRIEST

In the year 1496, four years after the discovery of America, a child was born to a Dutch peasant family living in the village of Witmarsum in the province of Friesland in the far northwest corner of continental Europe. The father, whose name was Simon, called his son, Menno, and according to the custom of the time the boy was called Menno Simons (Simon's Son.) The village of Witmarsum lies in a fertile plain, about halfway between the cities of Franeker and Bolsward, less than ten miles from the North Sea.

Quite early the parents of Menno Simons decided to consecrate their son to the service of the church, the Catholic Church, and in preparation for that service committed him to the care of a monastery near his home, possibly the Franciscan Monastery at Bolsward. Therefore long years he devoted himself to the spiritual exercises required of a monk, and to the traditional course of theological study required of candidates for the high office of the priesthood. During his years of study he learned to read and write Latin quite well, learned also to read the Greek, and became well acquainted with many ancient writings in Latin, particularly the writings of the church fathers such as Tertullian, Cyprian, and Eusebius. But the greatest book of all, the Bible, he failed utterly to read. It was not until two years after he was ordained to the priesthood that he ventured with great trepidation to open the covers of this forbidden volume.

Menno Simons' ordination to the Catholic priesthood took place in the month of March, 1524, in the twenty-eighth year of his life, probably at the city of Utrecht, seat of the ancient bishopric of Utrecht which included practically all of modern Holland in its jurisdiction. His first assignment was as parish priest in the village of Pingjum which lay next to his home village of Witmarsum. Here he served for a period of seven years, 1524-1531, as the second in rank of three parish priests. In 1531 Menno was transferred to his home village of Witmarsum where he served for five years as parish pastor until January, 1536, when he laid down his office in the Catholic Church and joined the small group of devoted evangelical brethren under the leadership of Obbe Philips, known as Anabaptists or Obbenites.

The twelve years of Menno Simons' service as a Catholic priest were outwardly spent, as far as man could see, in the performance of the usual round of duties of a Catholic priest in a small country village. He took his place in the regular worship of the church, performing the high ceremony of the mass as well as other rites and ceremonies. He offered prayers for the living and the dead, baptized the children of the parish, consecrated marriages, received confessions, administered discipline, and occasionally preached brief sermons in connection with the Sunday worship of the congregation. Like the typical village priest of the time he did not take his office nor his life very seriously. He gave little time or effort to study, but rather, as he himself confesses, joined his fellow priests in "playing cards, drinking, and frivolities of all sorts, as was the custom of such unfruitful men."

But outward appearances did not tell the full story of Menno's life during his twelve years in the priesthood. Very early, doubts about certain dogmas of the church arose to plague his conscience, and his life was made increasingly miserable by an inner soul-struggle which did not cease until he broke the bonds which bound him to the Catholic Church and stepped forth in the faith and liberty of the Gospel. Let us trace this eleven-year struggle.

In the very first year of Menno's priestly service, in 1525, the same year that Conrad Grebel and his brethren were founding the Mennonite Church in Zurich, Switzerland, a grave doubt arose to disturb his care-free, frivolous life with its formal religion. As he was celebrating the mass, suddenly the thought arose that possibly the bread and wine were not actually changed into the flesh and blood of the Lord as he had been taught, and as he was teaching the people. At first he shrank back from the thought as a whispering of the devil; but he could not get rid of the doubt, even by the use of the confessional. How Menno came to doubt the dogma of transubstantiation as held by the Catholic Church is not clear. He must have come in contact in some way with the teaching of Martin Luther or the other reformers on this point, either in books, or through the circulation of such ideas by word of mouth. As early as 1521 a Hollander by the name of Hoen had begun to teach the view that the elements used in the Lord's Supper were not actually transformed, but were merely symbols of the suffering and death of Christ. Whether Menno had read Hoen's writings or not, the rise of doubt on this point in his mind is evidence that the influence of the Reformation had already begun to reach into far-off Friesland, for the attitude toward the mass was a touchstone in the matter of the new evangelical heresy.

For about two years Menno was tormented by doubts regarding the mass before he found a way to help himself. He finally decided to seek relief by a diligent search of the New Testament. This decision was one of the greatest steps in Menno's life. In fact, it was the decisive step which was certain to lead to his final conversion, for the fundamental principle of the Reformation, indeed of the Gospel itself, was the sole authority of the Word of God as the source of truth for faith and life.

Now the decision of Menno Simons to search the Scripture for help in solving his doubts about the mass was not a decision to give up the authority of the church, for he probably hoped to find in Scripture a confirmation of the teaching of the church. The real problem came when Menno, having dared to open the lids of the Bible, discovered that it contained nothing of the traditional teaching of the church on the mass. By that discovery his inner conflict was brought to a climax, for he now was compelled to decide which of two authorities was to be supreme in his life, the church or the Holy Scriptures. He had been taught by the church that disbelief in its doctrine meant eternal death. What should he do? Fortunately, as Menno himself repeats, he found help in the writings of Martin Luther, for Martin Luther taught him that violation of the commandments of men could never lead to eternal death. It is not known in which of Luther's writings Menno found his help, possibly in the 1518 pamphlet, *Instruction on Several Articles,* or possibly in the important booklet written in 1520 entitled, *On the Freedom of a Christian Man.*

THE CATHOLIC PRIEST 5

When Menno Simons accepted Luther's view and dared to deny the dogma of transubstantiation as held by the Catholic Church because the Scriptures did not teach it, he found a way out of his doubts and struggles, a way to free his conscience and deliver his soul from eternal death. But in so doing he entered upon a road that would inevitably lead him out of the Catholic Church, for to follow the Scriptures in all matters of conscience was to forsake the fundamental principles of Catholicism. In making his decision on the mass, however, Menno did not follow Luther's teaching on this point; rather he developed his own interpretation of the Lord's Supper; he did not become a Lutheran in any way. What he was always grateful to Luther for, was the fundamental principle of the authority of Scripture as over against any human authority.

Menno's decision to follow the Scriptures was probably arrived at about the year 1528. It did not lead to his immediate abandonment of the Catholic Church, because at first he disagreed with the church only on the question of the mass, and no doubt thought that he could remain a loyal Catholic and teach his new view within the church. So like all the other Reformers he made no haste to change his church membership. Such a change would have meant giving up a good position with its generous income, and Menno still "loved the world, and the world him" too much, as he later said, to take such a radical step. The fact was that he was still far from a real comprehension of the Gospel, far from a spiritual conversion. The next years, from 1528-1531, were rather years of gradual enlightenment. He says of his own experience during this time, that "by the enlightenment and mercy of the Lord I increased in the knowledge of the Scriptures and soon was considered by a few, although undeservedly, as an evangelical preacher," that is as one who preached sermons based upon the Scriptures. Men began to seek him because "it was said that I preached the Word of God and was a good man."

Menno's progress in the Gospel was slow. One pillar of his Catholic faith had broken down, namely the mass, but he continued nevertheless, out of fear of men, to celebrate the mass as before. Outwardly he was still a loyal priest. He might never have left the Catholic Church had it not been that a second pillar in his Catholic faith also broke down, the pillar of baptism. The breaking down of this pillar was gradual. It is quite probable that it was begun by the reading of a small book by a certain Billican, a preacher in the South German city of Nördlingen, which advocated the principle of allowing liberty in the age of baptism. At least Menno refers to a book on baptism by certain preachers of Nördlingen. The book used arguments first given by Cyprian, one of the early Latin Church fathers of North Africa. At first Menno paid little attention to the question, but he was forced to think seriously about baptism in the year 1531 while he was still at Pingjum by a very strange occurrence in the neighboring city of Leeuwarden. On March 20, 1531, a certain tailor by the name of Sicke Freerks was publicly executed in that city for the strange reason that he had been baptized a second time. "It sounded strange in my ears," says Menno, "that a second baptism was spoken of." It seemed still more strange when Menno learned that Freerks was a pious, God-fearing man, who did not believe that the Scriptures taught that infants should be baptized but that they rather taught that baptism should be administered only to adults upon confession of a personal faith.

Freerks was an itinerant tailor who had been baptized in the city of Emden in East Friesland in the latter part of the year 1530 by a preacher named Jan Volkerts Trypmaker who had in turn been baptized and appointed lay preacher in the same city earlier in 1530 by a certain former Lutheran lay preacher named Melchior Hofmann. It has been claimed that Hofmann himself was baptized by certain radical Anabaptists in Strasbourg late in the year 1530. At any rate he began in 1530 to preach the new baptism and other similar doctrines of the Anabaptists, with Emden as his starting point. It should be said here that the main body of Anabaptists in Strasbourg, as well as in Switzerland and South Germany had never had anything to do with Hofmann. Indeed, in 1538, in a public disputation with leaders of the Reformed Church in Bern, Switzerland, certain Swiss Anabaptist leaders publicly repudiated all connection with Hofmann. Hofmann preached certain radical and fanatical doctrines relating to the second coming of Christ and the establishment of an earthly kingdom of God at Strasbourg, and also gave many strange interpretations to prophecy including the designation of himself as a second Enoch. The doctrines which he taught were clearly perversions of the Gospel, which he originated in his own fertile imagination, fanatical doctrines which he learned neither from Luther, nor Zwingli, nor the Anabaptists, nor any evangelical teachers. So Hofmann cannot be called an Anabaptist in the same sense as the Swiss Brethren or the

Mennonites, even though he taught baptism on confession of faith rather than infant baptism.

But Menno Simons knew nothing of all this when he heard about the execution of Sicke Freerks. What did mightily stir his thinking was the thought that one should be willing to die for the sake of a "second baptism." Was it possible that the Catholic Church was wrong in the matter of infant baptism just as it was wrong in the matter of the mass? Once again the priest Menno found himself in a conflict in his conscience due to the new doubt that had arisen. But this time he knew how to find the solution to his problem; as an "evangelical" preacher he turned at once to the Bible for light. Here, though he searched long, he "could find no report about infant baptism." He next turned for help to his superior at Pingjum, the pastor. The pastor finally admitted, after repeated discussions with Menno, that infant baptism had no basis in Scripture, but insisted that reason showed that it was necessary and justifiable. But Menno Simons, who had learned to trust the Word, was not willing "to trust his reason" alone. So he sought further for aid, this time searching diligently what the church fathers might have to say. They taught him that children needed baptism to be cleansed from original sin. But when Menno compared this teaching with the Scriptures he found a clear conflict, for did not the Scriptures teach that the blood of Christ the Redeemer, and not the water of baptism, was the only means for cleansing from sin? The church fathers were wrong.

As a last resort, Menno turned to his evangelical contemporaries, the reformers. All of them taught that children should be baptized, though for different reasons. Luther insisted that children could have faith, at least by proxy, and should be baptized on the basis of that faith; Butzer of Strasbourg urged that children be baptized as a guarantee that they would be reared in the ways of the Lord; while Bullinger of Zurich argued that children should be incorporated into the covenant people by baptism as the Jewish children had been incorporated into the covenant people by circumcision. But in spite of their various and diverse arguments, Menno noted that all alike failed to give Scriptural proof for infant baptism; each followed his own reason. Having arrived at the end of his diligent search with no proof that infant baptism was based on the Word of God, Menno concluded that "all were deceived about infant baptism,"— the Catholic Church, priests at Pingjum, the church fathers, the reformers—and that baptism on confession of faith alone was scriptural.

This momentous decision was the most significant one in Menno's entire career, for it sealed the breach with the Catholic Church and ultimately led him into the circle of the Anabaptists. Salvation by the sacrament of baptism was the cornerstone upon which the whole Catholic system of religion was built. One might conceivably remain a Catholic while denying transubstantiation, but how could one keep faith with a church whose essential mode of salvation was denied? On the other hand, the Anabaptists alone among the religious groups of the day denied the need for infant baptism and based membership in the church upon a personal experience of salvation of which water baptism was merely the outward symbol, so that Menno would some day find his way to them.

Yet this momentous decision, apparently arrived at in the year 1531, did not lead Menno at once to an outward breach with the church which he served as priest, and from which he drew his income. Five more years were to pass until this break came. Even though, as Menno asserts emphatically, his new beliefs in the matter of baptism (as well as the earlier change in the interpretation of the Lord's Supper) were received through the study of the Scripture under the guidance of the Holy Spirit, by the grace of God, his new-won convictions did not lead to action. There were, apparently, small groups of Anabaptists in the vicinity, but Menno did not associate himself with them. On the contrary when he was offered the promotion of an appointment to be pastor at Witmarsum, he did not hesitate to accept it. The larger income stirred his "lust for gain," says Menno, and so out of weakness, he continued to live the double life of a hypocrite, continued to officiate at the mass, continued to baptize infants. Menno himself gives the explanation of his weakness, for he says that although he had indeed a knowledge of the Scriptures it had been made fruitless by his fleshly life. What had changed his mind had not yet affected his heart, the Word of God was not yet living within him. He describes his hypocritical life at this time in harsh words: "Relying upon grace I did evil. I was as a carefully whitened sepulcher. Outwardly before men I was moral, chaste, generous; there was none that reproved my conduct; but inwardly I was full of dead men's bones . . . I sought mine own ease and my praise more zealously than Thy righteousness, honor, truth, and Thy Word."

The inconsistency between conviction and practice in the matter of baptism and the Lord's Supper did not let the new pastor at Witmarsum rest any more than it had the old priest at Pingjum. Menno's conscience constantly condemned him, he suffered under a continuous inner conflict.

The matter of baptism was stirred up afresh about a year after Menno's arrival in Witmarsum by the entrance of several Anabaptists into the community. Menno says that he neither saw the persons who "broke into the church in the matter of baptism," nor knew who they were, nor whence they came. Still Menno remained quiescent.

But finally a far more serious "break" into his parish occurred when certain ones of the "sect of Münster" reached Witmarsum, and "deceived many pious hearts in our village." This occurred sometime in the year 1534, for the revolutionary kingdom of Münster was not set up until February of that year.

The grievous error of the "perverted sect of Münster," as Menno repeatedly called them, was a very serious matter to Menno. Since the grievous damage wrought by the Münsterites was the final cause of Menno's withdrawal from Catholicism and his adherence to the Anabaptists, and since the fight against this fanatical movement with every weapon at his command was Menno's chief concern in the years 1534 and 1535, it is well to consider briefly the character and effects of Münsterism.

Jan Matthys, an unlearned but egotistical baker of Haarlem, Holland, was one of the small group of followers of Melchior Hofmann who had joined the "Melchiorites" about the year 1531. When Hofmann was cast into prison in Strasbourg in May, 1533, and consequently lost his leadership over his followers, certain unsavory elements in the movement began to win influence and gradually assumed the leadership. Among these Matthys was the chief. He was a powerful personality, filled with hate for the upper classes, and equipped with an imagination capable of devising the most fantastic schemes. He succeeded in wresting the leadership to himself and swinging most of the Melchiorites with him in a radical revolutionary program, although some like the brothers Obbe and Dirk Philips of Leeuwarden and others, totally rejected the strange new teachings of Matthys from the outset and absolutely refused to have anything to do with him even though they were threatened with persecution by his agents. In fact Obbe Philips took the leadership of a group of Melchiorites who definitely rejected all the radical teachings of Hofmann as well as the perversions of Matthys and sought to build their faith alone on a sound interpretation of Scripture.

Meanwhile Jan Matthys heard that the evangelical laboring classes of the city of Münster in Westphalia in northwest Germany had overthrown the dominant upper classes including the Catholic bishop. Thrilled with the thought that this might furnish him an opportunity to secure a base to begin his campaign against the "godless" upper classes, he at once sent agents to Münster who succeeded in winning over the evangelical preachers Rothmann and Roll to his program in January, 1534. Soon Matthys himself came to the city, took over control with the willing acquiescence of the fairly hysterical populace and promised to establish the kingdom of God on earth, the new Jerusalem. When he was killed in a sortie in April, Jan of Leiden took his place and installed himself as king. The amazing doctrine was now announced that since the kingdom of God had come, judgment was to be executed upon the unbelieving world by believers and members in the new kingdom. "Apostles" were sent out repeatedly from Münster inviting "believers" everywhere to come to the new Jerusalem and participate in its blessings. Thousands believed the announcement, accepted the invitation, and set out, and although many of them were arrested on the way, hundreds reached the city. However the reign of the Münster kingdom was not to be long; the siege of the city, which was instituted by the army of the Bishop of Münster in March, 1534, led to the final capture and the overthrow of the "Kingdom" in June, 1535, after terrible suffering and indescribable scenes of brutality within the kingdom.

Unfortunately the doctrine of vengeance and destruction of the ungodly by the godly had taken deep root in the circles of the former Melchiorites in Holland, so that lesser plottings and revolts were organized in other places outside of Münster, with consequent disaster. The terrible poison of the revolutionary fanaticism of Jan Matthys and Jan of Leiden wrought its deadly work among the harassed and persecuted Melchiorites of Holland.

Menno Simons came into contact with the "Münsterite perversion" sometime during the year 1534. Some of the more zealous and pious souls among his flock, doubtless some of those who had been influenced by his preaching and with whom he felt himself spiritually united, were swept away into the fanaticism of the Münsterite error. Even his own brother was among the number. Although Menno had been inclined to adopt the principle of adult baptism, he could not for a moment think of casting his lot with the Münsterites. He admitted that they had a commendable zeal, but declared that they erred grievously in their teaching. He was deeply distressed as he saw their abominable doctrines making inroads among the pious of his parish and determined to throw himself heart and soul into the struggle against them.

The fight against the Münsterite influence occupied Menno's chief attention for almost a year. He was so vigorous in his public denunciation of them in his sermons that he soon won the reputation of being able "to stop the mouths of the enemy very well." In his pastoral visits he sought not only to hold those who were in danger, but to win back those who had already been deceived and had slipped. He even succeeded in having one secret and one public meeting with "two fathers of the perverted sect." Finally Menno decided to carry the battle against them still further by writing. The result of his endeavors was a little pamphlet, written probably early in 1535, although printed for the first time in 1627, bearing the title: "A Clear and Indubitable Proof from Holy Scripture Against the Abominable and Great Blasphemy of Jan van Leiden." In this writing Menno vigorously attacked the claims of "King" Jan to divine authority, and proved that the taking of arms by the Münsterites was a gross sin and contrary to the will of God for the church, as well as contrary to the example and spirit of Christ. He appealed to all true Christians everywhere to separate themselves from such abominations and to follow after the example of Christ.

CHAPTER II

CONVERSION AND RENUNCIATION OF CATHOLICISM 1535-1536

But even while Menno was fighting vigorously the good fight of truth against the error of the Münsterites, he was becoming constantly more deeply involved in a serious inner conflict. He sought to keep the pious souls who were dissatisfied with the Catholic Church from following the heresy of the Münsterites, but unless he provided them with something better, did he not seem to be merely a defender and supporter of the Catholic Church? And when his Catholic friends used his name and arguments to strike down the Münsterites was he not letting himself appear to be their ally in maintaining the rule of darkness in that church? The more successfully he fought the Münsterites the more intolerable the situation became to his conscience.

The climax of the conflict in his soul came with the tragedy at the Old Cloister near Bolsward when almost three hundred misguided souls lost their lives, among them his own brother in the flesh. The group was one of those referred to earlier, which had been imbued with the poison of the Münsterite revolution, and had decided to set up its own city of refuge and begin its own campaign for the kingdom of God in Friesland. In March, 1535, a large company of three hundred had seized an old monastery (Oude Kloster) outside of the city of Bolsward and entrenched itself therein. They were unable to hold out long against the siege of the forces of the government and after one hundred thirty had been slain, the rest were captured and executed on April 7th. The sight of these "poor misguided sheep," as Menno called them, giving their blood and their lives for their faith, even though it was a false faith, made an extraordinary impression upon Menno. He could not cast it off. They had given their lives for error, while he was not willing to give anything for the truth, but merely for fear of losing his reputation and his income continued to be a part of a system which his conscience had rejected. If he had had the courage to come out into the open, renounce Catholic doctrine and practices, and be a shepherd to these erring sheep, perhaps he could have saved them and averted the tragedy. Their blood, he felt, was upon his soul, and there it burned deeply to his shame. "The blood of these people," he said, "became such a burden to me that I could not endure it nor find rest in my soul." It was true that he had spoken against some of the abominations of the papal system, but out of fear of the "cross of his Lord" he had not made a clean breach with the whole system.

The tragedy of the Old-Cloisterites brought Menno to the parting of the ways; he now saw clearly his duty. As a servant of God he could not evade the responsibility to help the erring sheep, and as one who professed obedience and trust in God he dared no longer refuse to take up the cross of persecution and suffering whatever the cost might be. He could no longer go against his conscience and conviction.

In this extremity of his soul, Menno turned to God with sighing and tears, pleading for grace and forgiveness, pleading for a pure heart and courage to preach His holy name and His Word in all truth. In his own account

RENUNCIATION OF CATHOLICISM

of his conversion Menno describes his change of heart in the following words: "My heart trembled in my body. I prayed God with sighs and tears that He would give me, a troubled sinner, the gift of His grace and create a clear heart in me, that through the merits of the crimson blood of Christ He would graciously forgive my unclean walk and ease-seeking life, and bestow upon me wisdom, candor and courage, that I might preach His exalted and adorable name and Holy Word unadulterated and make manifest His truth to His praise." The Lord was gracious unto him, the decision was made, and Menno went forth with a sense of divine mission to a new life. Some may criticise Menno for having tarried so long with his decision, but such condemnation is hardly just. The full light dawned upon him but gradually and his was a slow moving Frisian nature, not easily stirred and changed. What is important to note is that once Menno was stirred he was moved to the depths of his nature, and from that decision once made he never turned back. The change was so deep, so thorough, so complete, and gave him such a sense of divine mission, that he was enabled by the grace of God to be an inspired leader, a mighty tower of strength to his bitterly persecuted people for more than twenty-five years. In reality, a comparison with Luther and Zwingli casts no discredit upon Menno Simons in respect to the speed of his break with Rome, particularly when we remember that Martin Luther had the powerful protection of the Elector of Saxony and endangered neither his reputation nor his income by his change, while Zwingli never moved until he had the support of the city council of Zurich, whose well-paid pastor he remained until his death on the field of Cappell.

MENNO SIMONS' LIFE AND WRITINGS

Menno Simons' decision to break completely with the Catholic Church probably occurred in April, 1535, soon after the tragedy at Bolsward. He began at once to preach openly from his pulpit in Witmarsum the truths which he had possibly taught in part in private earlier, the word of repentance, of true faith, of believers' baptism, of the right Lord's Supper. He dared now to attack openly all the evils of the church, for he was done with all calculations to save himself. He apparently determined to use the Witmarsum church as the platform for his new message as long as possible, as Luther had done at Wittenberg, and Zwingli at Zurich. The marvel is that for nine months he was permitted to do this, according to his own statement. During these nine months he carried on a double campaign, on the one hand he was striving mightily to save his people from the Münsterite abominations, and on the other hand he was seeking to lead them out of their old beliefs into the true faith of the Gospel. Note his own description of his attitude and activity during these nine months.

> "In consequence, I began in the name of the Lord to preach publicly from the pulpit the word of true repentance, to direct the people unto the narrow path and with the power of the Scriptures to reprove all sin and ungodliness, all idolatry and false worship, and to testify to the true worship, also baptism and the Lord's Supper according to the teaching of Christ, to the extent that I at that time had received grace from God. I also faithfully warned every one of the Münsterite abominations, viz., king, polygamy, earthly kingdom, the sword, etc., until after about nine months when the gracious Lord granted me His fatherly Spirit, aid, power and help, that I voluntarily forsook my good name, honor and reputation which I had among men and renounced all the abominations of Antichrist, mass, infant baptism and

my unprofitable life, and willingly submitted to homelessness and poverty under the cross of my Lord Jesus Christ; in my weakness I feared God, sought out the pious and, although they were few in number, I found some who had a commendable zeal and maintained the truth.

"Behold thus, my reader, the God of mercy, through His abounding grace which He bestowed upon me, a miserable sinner, has first touched my heart, given me a new mind, humbled me in His fear, taught me in part to know myself, turned me from the way of death and graciously called me into the narrow path of life, into the communion of His saints. To Him be praise forevermore. Amen."

But Menno's position as an evangelical preacher in a Catholic pulpit and parish could not long be maintained. His complete secession from the church was only a matter of time. Just when he was baptized is not clear, possibly soon after his conversion in April, but more probably not until his public secession from the church nine months later. During these nine months he may have introduced changes in the ceremonies and sacraments of the church as well as in the content of his preaching. It is possible that the mass was changed into a simple communion service in commemoration of the Savior's suffering and death, and certainly all infant baptisms must have ceased. Finally it became apparent to Menno that he could no longer have any connection with the old church, with "Babel," even in a purely external way. Consequently he voluntarily, without compulsion, "forsook Babel and entered the true church, the house of his Lord." This he did by relinquishing his pulpit and his charge as a priest and by leaving the village of Witmarsum for other residence. The exact time of the renunciation of the papal church was probably Sunday, January 30, 1536. It may be assumed that he went to Obbe Philips in Leeuwarden to tell him of his decision, for Menno says that he first looked about him for God-fearing people.

But for the next few months after his secession what Menno wanted more than anything else was quiet to think over the implications of his decision, to read the Word of God and to meditate upon it, and to solve some of the theological questions which still troubled him. One of these questions concerned the exact mode of the incarnation. He had apparently learned of some peculiar views of the incarnation from some of the brethren, who may have gotten it originally from Melchior Hofmann, and wanted to decide for himself what he should believe. The problem which disturbed him was this: How could the sinless divine nature of Christ be incarnated in the flesh of sinful descendants of fallen Adam? Because of his earnest desire for the truth and his great fear of unbelief and error, Menno came into a serious conflict on this question. He fasted and prayed to God "that He might reveal to him the mystery of the conception of His blessed Son" insofar as this was necessary for the glory of God and the lightening of the burden of his conscience. Attempts to secure help from the brethren were unsatisfactory. After several months Menno felt that he had come to a satisfying conclusion on this question by adopting a theory of the incarnation which made the incarnation a new creation of the human flesh of Christ in Mary so that Christ took being *in* Mary but was not born of Mary's flesh. It was similar to Hofmann's view. Menno developed this theory chiefly to satisfy himself, and seldom said much about it except when he was forced to do

RENUNCIATION OF CATHOLICISM

so in public debates by his enemies who found his peculiar view of the incarnation a weak spot. He complained repeatedly that he was compelled against his inclination to debate on this point. It is of interest to note that Menno's vagary on the mode of the incarnation was not acceptable to the Swiss Mennonites, and that although it continued to have influence on the thinking of some of the Dutch-North German Mennonites this theory of the incarnation never found its way into any authoritative creed or confession of the Mennonite Church.

The year following Menno's public renunciation of the Catholic Church in January, 1536, was spent in retirement, as has been stated above. Apparently Menno did not remain at any one place. Traces of his movements during this time have been preserved in the records of martyrs who were punished several years later for sheltering him. He traveled from Witmarsum to Leeuwarden, back to Witmarsum and to Groningen. Toward the end of the year he seems to have settled down in a retreat in or near the city of Groningen in northeast Holland, for according to an old tradition it was here that he was ordained as an elder or bishop.

Menno fails to mention the place of his ordination or the names of those who ordained him, but tells in detail the experience which led up to the final commission. It must be clear of course that after his secession Menno had continued to preach and to teach as he had occasion and opportunity; but he had assumed no definite responsibility or leadership among the Brethren since leaving Witmarsum. While he was giving himself to study and writing in his retreat near Groningen, six or eight of the brethren came to him and entreated him to accept the office of elder or chief shepherd and bishop of the brotherhood. The time of the call was "about a year after he left the papacy," that is, sometime during the winter of 1536-1537. It was not easy for Menno to accept the call, for although he considered it his duty to aid in shepherding the "God-fearing ones," yet he knew what might await him out in the world if he should publicly appear as their leader. So he asked for time for prayer and consideration. When the brethren soon after repeated the call a second time, Menno yielded, though not without a struggle. He describes his decision thus:

> "When I heard this [the call] my heart was greatly troubled. Apprehension and fear was on every side. For on the one hand I saw my limited talents, my great lack of knowledge, the weakness of my nature, the timidity of my flesh, the very great wickedness, wantonness, perversity and tyranny of the world, the mighty great sects [the persecuting state churches], the subtlety of many men and the indescribably heavy cross which, if I began to preach, would be the more felt; and on the other hand I recognized the pitifully great hunger, want and need of the God-fearing, pious souls, for I saw plainly that they erred as innocent sheep which have no shepherd.
>
> "When the persons before mentioned did not desist from their entreaties, and my own conscience made me uneasy in view of the great hunger and need already spoken of, I consecrated myself, soul and body to the Lord, and committed myself to His gracious leading, and I began in due time [i. e., after having been ordained to the ministry of the Word] according to His holy Word to teach and to baptize, to labor with my limited talents in the harvest field of the Lord, to assist in building up His holy city and temple and to repair the dilapidated walls."

RENUNCIATION OF CATHOLICISM

The ordination must have taken place early in 1537, and was almost certainly performed by Obbe Philips.

The significance of Menno's acceptance of the leadership of the brotherhood in northern Holland, known at that time as Obbenites, can scarcely be overestimated. As Menno himself says, the few who had remained faithful to scriptural, evangelical doctrines under the leadership of Obbe and Dirk Philips, and had resisted the temptation to follow after the fanatical doctrines of Jan Matthys, were discouraged and scattered, eagerly looking for a strong leader. Obbe Philips himself finally lost heart, laid down his office as bishop, and left the Brotherhood entirely a few years later, probably in 1541. Many of those who had been swept away in the Münsterite stream, disillusioned by the tragic failure of the "Kingdom", were helplessly confused as sheep without a shepherd. They perhaps could be won back to a Gospel faith.

On the other hand other fanatical leaders were still trying to promote radical movements in spite of the collapse of Münster, and they were endangering the faith of many. Chief among them was Jan of Batenburg, the outstanding leader, whose program of violent vengeance degenerated more and more into simple banditry. A gathering of these revolutionary Anabaptists was held at Bocholt in Westphalia in August, 1536. Even David Joris, whom Obbe Philips had ordained as a bishop about the same time as he ordained Menno, turned out to be an ecstatic and visionary fanatic, whose foolish interpretations of Scripture were matched by his unclean and hypocritical character. It is not too much to say that the preservation of the Dutch and North German Anabaptists from complete annihilation or at least from absorption into the fanaticism of the Batenburgers and Davidians, and their rallying around a Biblical standard of faith and life, was due in large measure to the fruitful labors of Menno Simons, who yielded to the earnest appeal of his God-fearing brethren and in so doing yielded himself heart and body and soul to his God, and took upon himself "the heavy cross" of his Lord in a faithful, unremitting devoted ministry until his death at Wüstenfelde in Holstein in 1561.

CHAPTER III

LABORS IN HOLLAND 1536-1543

The field of labor assigned to Menno Simons at the time of his ordination was apparently not limited in any way. He was expected to visit the scattered brethren, to preach, to baptize, to build up the church of God as he had opportunity. Naturally he sought to fulfill his task first in the territory which lay near at hand. Very little direct evidence of his work during the first years of his ministry has been preserved. What is available shows that although he was married to a certain Gertrude in 1536 or 1537, he maintained no permanent residence, but traveled about a great deal. His first field of labor extended from East Friesland, where he baptized a certain Peter Jans at Oldersum in 1536, westward across the two northern provinces of Groningen and West Friesland. In the latter two provinces he spent most of his time until 1541.

Menno himself tells of one man whom he had baptized in West Friesland and who was executed Jan. 8, 1539, because he had sheltered Menno.

"About the year 1539," writes Menno, "a very pious and God-fearing man named Tjard Reynders was apprehended in the place where I sojourned, for the reason that he had received me, a homeless man, out of compassion and love, into his house, although in secret. A short time after this he was, after a free confession of his faith, executed and broken on the wheel as a valiant soldier of Christ, according to the example of his Lord, although he had the testimony, even of his enemies, that he was an unblamable and pious man."

It is noteworthy that in this statement Menno calls himself a homeless man. He came to West Friesland several times a year until 1541, and was so effective in his work that he soon became known as the outstanding leader of the Anabaptists in the province. The provincial authorities had tried unsuccessfully for several years to extirpate "the accursed sect" and finally concluded that they would have no success until Menno himself was gotten out of the way. A plan was proposed to Mary, regent of the Netherlands, by which certain captured Anabaptists might be prevailed upon to betray Menno in return for pardon, but it failed to work. The letter, dated May 19, 1541, in which the plan was outlined, illustrates vividly the dangers which faced Menno in his labors.

"Most serene, right honorable, most mighty Queen, most gracious Lady. We offer ourselves as humbly as we can for Your Majesty's service. Most gracious Lady, although the error of the cursed sect of the Anabaptists which in the last five or six years has very strongly prevailed in this land of Friesland, but now—the Lord be praised—through the publication of divers placards and through executions which have been carried into effect against transgressors of that sort, this sect would doubtless be and remain extirpated, were it not that a former priest Menno Symonsz who is one of the principal leaders of the aforesaid sect and about three or four years ago became fugitive, has roved about since that time once or twice a year in these parts and has misled many simple and innocent people. To seize and apprehend this man we have offered a large sum of money, but until now with no success. Therefore we have entertained the thought of offering and promising pardon and mercy to a few who have been misled (by the Anabaptists) and who desire grace (having recanted their faith) if they would bring about the imprisonment of the said Menno Symons. However we would not be so bold as to do this ourselves but desire first to advise Your Majesty of it, praying to be informed of Your Majesty's good pleasure and command which we, to the extent of our power, are willing and ready to carry out, as knows God Almighty. May He long spare Your Majesty in good health and happy reign. Written at Leeuwarden on the nineteenth day of May, 1541. Your Majesty's very humble and obedient servants, the counsellors ordained of the Imperial Majesty in Friesland."

The offers of reward for Menno's arrest which had been announced by placards spread throughout the province of West Friesland brought no results, nor did they deter Menno from his labors in that region. At last the Emperor himself, Charles V, was prevailed upon to publish a severe edict against Menno on Dec. 7, 1542, which placed a price of 100 gold guilders on his head, and which further forbade giving aid or shelter to him in any way or reading his books. All his followers were likewise ordered to be arrested. Whoever should succeed in delivering Menno to the authorities was promised pardon for any crime which he might have committed.

The severity of this edict indicates the intensity of the persecution which Menno and his followers experienced in Friesland at this time. Menno was fully aware of the danger which faced him but he continued to labor with unabated zeal and courage. His spirit is well characterized by the following lines from a tract which he wrote about this time:

"And above all pray for your poor and willing minister who is sought with great diligence to be delivered up to death, that God, the gracious Father, may strengthen him with His Holy Spirit and save him from the hands of those who so unjustly seek his life, if it be His Fatherly will; and if it be not His will, that He may then grant him in all tribulation, torture, suffering, persecution and death such heart, mind, wisdom and strength," etc.

In the year 1541 Menno shifted his field of labor further south to the city of Amsterdam and the territory immediately surrounding it known as the province of North Holland. Here he spent most of his time for the two years from 1541 to 1543, without breaking off his contacts with Friesland and Groningen. While he doubtless baptized many in Amsterdam and vicinity during this time, the names of but two have been preserved, Lukas Lamberts and the bookseller Jan Claeszoon. Both were executed as martyrs on January 19, 1544, shortly after Menno left this region. Claeszoon or Claassen circulated Menno's writings and possibly even published some of them. He was also an ordained minister.

During the seven years of labor in the Netherlands Menno was quite active in writing, and in circulating the booklets which he wrote. A total of seven titles appeared, five of which were rather small pamphlets, varying in size from twenty to sixty pages of average book size. The two most important books were *The Foundation of Christian Doctrine,* a book of two hundred fifty pages written in 1539, and *Of the True Christian Faith,* a book of one hundred sixty pages also written in 1541. *Christian Baptism,* a book of sixty pages published in 1539, is also of importance. All of the writings of this period of Menno's life are substantial doctrinal expositions dealing with fundamental doctrines such as repentance, faith, the new birth, holiness, and similar themes. They are not learned treatises but rather simply written books well-adapted to the common man, and deal with the great issues of the hour. For this reason they were widely read and did splendid service in strengthening the faith of many who were disturbed and unsettled by the many conflicting currents of the day. It is no wonder that the authorities were so anxious to suppress Menno's writings, and that they placed severe penalties upon those who read them or distributed them.

CHAPTER IV

LABORS IN NORTHWEST GERMANY 1543-1546

Feeling that a wider field of service was open to him in northwest Germany where the severe edicts of the Emperor and the regent were not in force, Menno left Holland permanently in the fall of 1543 after seven years of arduous and fruitful labors there. The remaining eighteen years of his life till his death in 1561 he devoted to building up the church in northwest Germany, the territory just immediately east of Holland. The comparative length of his labors in the two countries shows that Menno was less of a Hollander than a German during his twenty-five years of service as a Mennonite bishop, a fact which has seldom been recognized as it should. Persecution was not so severe in the territories of northwest Germany as in Holland, first because the Emperor, who was a staunch Catholic, had very little power or influence here, and second because many of the rulers and lesser nobility were inclined to be tolerant. Menno's life in Germany falls into three unequal periods which will be treated successively; (1) a few months in East Friesland, 1543-1544, (2) two years in the bishopric of Cologne, 1544-1546, (3) fifteen years in Holstein and the Baltic seacoast region.

In the early winter of 1543-1544, Menno with his family appeared in East Friesland where the Countess Anna was reigning, of which the capital was the seacoast town of Emden. At this time the territory was in transition from Catholicism to Protestantism, so the Anabaptists were temporarily tolerated. Anna had just appointed (1543) John a 'Lasco, a Zwinglian reformer and native of Poland who had been active in the province since 1540, to organize the proposed new Protestant state church. Just where Menno settled when he came to East Friesland is unknown, except that it was not in Emden, although there was apparently a fair-sized congregation of brethren here which had been established under the leadership of Obbe and Dirk Philips.

Because of the tolerance of the ruler, Countess Anna, several sects had found refuge in East Friesland in addition to the "Mennonites." Among them were the Batenburgers, who as followers of Jan van Batenburg still held to the bloody doctrines of Münster, and the Davidians, followers of that strange visionary fanatic, David Joris, a former coworker of the Philips brothers who had separated from them in 1536. When John a 'Lasco entered upon his work as the reformer of East Friesland in 1543 he soon became aware of the difference between the fanatical, revolutionary sects and the peaceful, relatively orthodox Mennonites. Being seriously concerned with the development of a sound and just policy toward all he was very glad to learn through some of the brethren of the arrival of Menno Simons himself as the leader in the province, and invited him to come to the capital for a discussion of theological questions. This discussion, called by some a debate or disputation although it really was more of a semipublic interview, was held with the consent of the ruler January 28-31, 1544, in the chapel of the former Franciscan monastery in Emden. Several Reformed ministers and others were present. Three days were necessary to cover the field of discussion, which included the following topics: the incarnation of Christ, baptism, original sin, and the calling of ministers. On two subjects, original sin and sanctification, Menno and a 'Lasco agreed; on the remaining three no agreement was possible. Menno himself testifies that he was treated with kindness, and that the only demand made was that he submit a written statement of his faith which might be presented to the authorities so that they might have definite and reliable information concerning the principles which Menno and his followers upheld.

The promised statement of faith was delivered by Menno three months later with the title, *Brief and Clear Confession and Scriptural Instruction*. It dealt at length (about seventy pages) with two of the disputed doctrines, the incarnation and the calling of ministers, and promised a further statement later on baptism, the third point. The later statement was never given, and a 'Lasco proceeded to publish Menno's statement of principles without his consent. He intended to use it as a weapon against the Mennonites, whereas Menno had hoped by it to win recognition or at least tolerance. A 'Lasco published a reply in the form of a book written in Latin, which appeared at Bonn the following year, 1545. Years later, in 1554, Menno replied in turn in a book of about one hundred pages entitled, *Clear, Incontrovertible Confession and Demonstration*.

A 'Lasco's attitude toward the Mennonites was somewhat mixed. He undoubtedly advised the authorities not to permit the leaders such as Menno to remain in the territory, yet he seemed to be willing to grant a measure of toleration to the ordinary members, and took care to distinguish them from such radical groups as the Batenburgers. When Countess Anna in 1544 under pressure from Holland issued an edict banishing all "Anabaptists," a 'Lasco persuaded her to modify it so as to expel the radicals and permit the "Menists" milder treatment involving examination by a 'Lasco, although ultimate banishment was also indicated. This modified decree of 1545 is of historic interest as the first document in which the name "Menist" or Mennonite was used to refer to the followers of Menno Simons.

Before the middle of the year 1544, probably in May, Menno fled from East Friesland to find refuge and peace in the territory of the bishopric of Cologne. Two reasons probably drew Menno to the Rhineland. One was the existence in this territory of a number of flourishing congregations of the Brethren. The other was the very tolerant policy of Archbishop Herman von Wied, who was favorable to the Reformation and who was at that time engaged in transforming the bishopric into a Lutheran principality.

The two years (1544-1546) which Menno was permitted to spend in the bishopric of Cologne until Herman von Wied was driven out by his Catholic enemies in 1546, were among the most peaceful and fruitful of his life. The few traces of his labors and movements which have been preserved reveal that he traveled a great deal, that his books were widely distributed and read, and that his name and fame were growing rapidly. In his own writings Menno later refers to some of his experiences here, mentioning the fact that he had been invited to discuss theological matters with the preachers at Bonn on the Rhine and also with the preachers at Wesel in the territory of Cleve. At Bonn the authorities, influenced by reports from John a

'Lasco and his friend, Hardenberg, finally rejected the plan, while the Wesel preachers in their reply to Menno's offer to come, offered to let the hangman instruct Menno, although they had previously told one of Menno's friends that they would be ready to meet him in a discussion.

Traces of Menno's labors in the Rhineland have been preserved in the confessions and testimonies of some of the martyrs. Among the places mentioned where he preached are Fischerswert and Illekhoven. At the latter place Menno lodged in 1545 with a deacon named Lemke. One martyr was executed because he had transported Menno Simons and two other men in a boat from his home at Fischerswert down the Meuse River to Roermond. When the mild reign of Archbishop Herman came to an end by his deposition because of the defeat of the Protestant princes in the Smalcald War in 1546, and Catholicism was restored throughout the province, Menno's time in Cologne was up and he was forced to flee.

CHAPTER V

LABORS IN HOLSTEIN 1546-1561

Forced to leave the Rhineland, Menno fled with his sick wife and small children to the territory of Holstein which lay east and north of Hamburg along the Baltic seacoast. Already small groups of Mennonites fleeing from persecution in Holland had found their way into this region which was under the sovereignty of the king of Denmark and thus not under the anti-Anabaptist laws of the empire. Where Menno first settled is unknown, although he did live for a time in the city of Wismar; his later residence was in or near the small village of Wüstenfelde not far from Oldesloe, about halfway between the Hanseatic cities of Hamburg and Lübeck. The first evidence of Menno's presence in Holstein was his participation in a theological discussion at Lübeck in 1546 with Nicholas Blesdijk, a son-in-law and follower of the notorious David Joris, and a leader of the sect of Davidians.

David Joris, a Fleming born at Bruges, was one of the most remarkable, and notorious characters which the Reformation produced. He early became a zealous Lutheran, but in 1531 came under the influence of Melchior Hofmann's teachings and joined the group of Melchiorites. Later he associated with the Obbenites and was apparently ordained a minister by Obbe Philips before Menno Simons joined the group. However, when Joris became infected with Münsterite ideas and developed fanatical tendencies, which was apparently in the year 1536, the Obbenites disowned him. From that time on

Joris led a movement of his own which became known as the Davidians, although his following never became large. Finally in 1544 under the stress of persecution and tribulation he forsook his followers, assumed the name of John of Bruges, and settled as a Reformed refugee in Basel where he died in 1556.

The teachings of Joris were a strange mixture of theological fanaticism and antinomianism. He claimed to have a divine call to be a prophet and to establish the kingdom of God on earth over which he was to reign as the third David. He went so far as to teach that the work and revelation of Christ were not adequate and that the Holy Scriptures were to be superseded by his own literally inspired writings which contained the final revelation of God. His conception of fleshly sin was such that he taught that the inner man was not affected by what the flesh might do, and that hence the gross works of the flesh were not to be counted as sin. As a consequence of such teaching, much sin and immorality, including adultery and polygamy, appeared among the Davidians.

Menno had openly attacked David Joris and his teachings in his very first writings, 1536-1539. Aroused by Menno's attack in the *Foundation,* Joris wrote a letter to Menno challenging him to prepare for a great battle. Menno replied vigorously to the challenge in a strong letter to Joris written in 1542, in which he pointed out that further contact between the two men was impossible because they stood on radically different platforms, since Menno followed Christ and His word, whereas Joris followed his own foolish and egotistical dreams and hallucinations. He therefore requested Joris to cease writing to him, for he would not read any more of his writings until he had learned to respect and honor the word of Christ.

When Joris disappeared from the world of affairs under the alias of John of Bruges, an end was put to the personal conflict, but not to contact between Menno and the Davidian. In a country place near Lübeck Menno engaged in an extended discussion with the above-mentioned Nicholas Blesdijk, in which baptism and other questions were debated. Menno was supported in the debate by Dirk Philips, Leonard Bouwens, Gillis of Aachen, and Adam Pastor. The record of the discussion was printed but seems to have been lost. However Blesdijk describes the meeting in several of his books, especially in one published in 1546 under the title, *A Christian Vindication and Refutation . . . of a Letter Written by Menno Simons*. Among the many points of difference between the Mennonites and the Davidians, one stands out sharply. Menno and his brethren held that the doctrine of the church and its correct organization and discipline was one of the most important doctrines of Christianity, whereas the Davidians would have nothing of the sort. For them the individual and a so-called "Spiritual" interpretation of the Scriptures was the center and source of Christian doctrine.

The presence of the four brethren in the debate at Lübeck with Blesdijk, suggests organized co-operation among the leaders of the Mennonites at this time. There is good evidence to believe that about this time the bishops began to have occasional meetings or conferences, and that they worked out a plan of co-operation whereby a definite territory was assigned to each bishop within which he was permanently responsible for pastoral oversight, for discipline, and for baptizing new converts. Bouwens was given the West (Holland), Gillis of Aachen received the Rhineland, Dirk Philips was assigned the region of Danzig and its vicinity along the eastern Baltic, while Menno retained the central district from East Friesland to Holstein and was recognized as the chief among the bishops. Dirk Philips was apparently a bishop before Menno was ordained in 1536. Gillis of Aachen was ordained a bishop about 1542, while Bouwens was not made a bishop until 1551. Unfortunately, the first leader of the brethren, Obbe Philips, had lost heart about 1541 and turned back upon the movement which he had served so well. Menno considered him an apostate.

The bishops mentioned above, together with others, met occasionally at various places. At such meetings reports were given of conditions in the various fields, problems were discussed, serious cases of discipline decided, and regulations drawn up for the church. The meeting in Lübeck in 1546 on the occasion of the debate with Blesdijk is the first recorded meeting of the sort. At least two meetings were held in the next year, 1547, one in Emden and one in Goch. The chief matter considered at these meetings was the doctrinal error which had become apparent in the teaching of Adam Pastor (Roelof Martens), one of the leaders who had been ordained about 1542 by Menno Simons and Dirk Philips. Pastor erred in the doctrine of the divinity of Christ, for he held that Christ did not exist as the Son of God previous to His coming into the world, and was divine after His incarnation only in the sense that God dwelled in Him. He accepted the authority of the Bible as the Word of God but sought to find support for his heresy by certain peculiar interpretations. At the first meeting in 1547 in Emden the bishops still entertained hope that Pastor might be restored to his former doctrinal position. However, the hoped-for change for the better did not appear so that at a second meeting held in the same year at Goch, Pastor was excommunicated. Pastor himself held Menno jointly responsible for the excommunication, although Dirk Philips was apparently the one who spoke the words of the ban in the name of the group.

At first Pastor succeeded in securing a following and making some trouble in the church. To counteract the influence of his teaching, Menno in 1550 wrote a tract on the deity of Christ called, *Confession of the Triune God.* In no uncertain tones he set forth the scriptural teaching on this subject, and warned the church strongly against the new teaching as a violation of a fundamental doctrine of the Gospel. The tract, a pamphlet of about twenty pages, was first circulated among some of the churches in handwritten form. Later a copy made for the brethren in Groningen was printed.

The last contact between Menno Simons and Adam Pastor was at a debate at Lübeck in 1552. The purpose of the original excommunication in 1547 had been twofold, first to protect the church, and second to make the man consider the error of his ways with the hope that he might be won back. With the hope that Pastor might be persuaded to return, Menno agreed to the discussion in 1552. According to Pastor's own report of the meeting the discussion was fruitless. Little further is heard of the followers of Pastor. After a period of activity in the Rhineland and Westphalia, Pastor died in Münster. His following, which never was large, gradually disintegrated.

It has been said above that Menno's assignment as a bishop involved the pastoral oversight of the entire territory in northern Germany east of Groningen to Prussia, including East Friesland, Oldenburg, Holstein, Mecklenburg and possibly Pomerania. His travels at times took him outside of these territories. In 1547 he attended the meeting of the elders in Goch; in April, 1549 he was in West Friesland near Leeuwarden; and in the summer of 1549 he visited the brethren in Prussia. The visit to Prussia is reported by Menno himself in a letter to the brethren in Prussia dated Oct. 7, 1549. The letter consists primarily of an appeal to maintain the peace and unity which had been restored among the brethren after a serious controversy had been settled by Menno during his visit in the previous summer.

Scarcely had Menno returned from settling the controversy in Prussia until he found it necessary to make a trip to the western congregations in a similar mission. The influence of Pastor's heretical teaching concerning the deity of Christ was still making trouble, and other disputes had arisen over the application of the ban in matters of excommunication. On both subjects Menno wrote pamphlets in the year 1550. The one against Pastor has already been mentioned; the second pamphlet was entitled *A Clear Discussion of Excommunication*. This latter writing, a pamphlet of about forty-five pages, was circulated among the churches in handwritten form. It was not printed until 1597. The pamphlet was a discussion of the function, practice and extent of the ban, and was directed against those who wished it applied to spiritual matters only. In the course of the western trip a conference was held at Emden in 1549 at which among other things, one of the ministers, Francis Kuyper, was excommunicated by Menno because of having defended unscriptural views on justification by faith and other points.

Aside from these two briefer pamphlets of 1550 (which were not printed at once) and a few short letters and four brief petitions written in 1551 and 1552, Menno did not publish anything of importance between 1541 and 1554, except the *Reply to Gellius Faber* in 1552, a book of about two hundred fifty pages. One reason was perhaps that he was too busy in his travels and in performing his duties as a bishop to have much time for writing. Another reason may have been the difficulty in finding a printer who would print his books for him. The four petitions mentioned above were addressed in a general way to the civil authorities and to the learned men and teachers of the Lutheran and Reformed state churches of Germany. The purpose of all the "petitions" was to refute the charges of heresy and fanaticism which were constantly being brought against the Mennonites by their enemies. In them Menno asserted in the strongest possible terms that he and his brethren had no connection whatsoever with Münster, and that their only purpose was to be truly Biblical Christian believers. He also appealed for public discussions in which he would have an opportunity to refute the false accusations of his enemies.

The *Reply to Gellius Faber* mentioned above was a lengthy discussion of six fundamental questions: the calling of ministers, baptism, Lord's Supper, ban, church, and incarnation. Faber, a Reformed minister in Emden, associate of a 'Lasco, had attacked the doctrines of the Mennonites, although not specifically directing his attack against Menno. This book is Menno's largest, though of little importance because it merely repeats the thought of his earlier writings. The most important thing in it is his account of his own conversion and call to the ministry, which has often been reprinted as a separate tract.

During the winter 1553-1554 Menno spent some time in the Hanseatic city of Wismar on the Baltic seacoast between Lübeck and Rostock. Here he fellowshipped with a Mennonite congregation, although he endeavored to keep his place of residence hidden. In spite of the attempt to maintain secrecy he became involved in a very interesting fashion in a theological discussion with two Reformed ministers. It came about in this way. A boatload of Reformed refugees from London who had been driven out of England by persecution, arrived off the harbor of Wismar on December 21, 1553. The Mennonites of the city were the only ones willing to help the needy refugees whose ship had frozen fast in the ice some distance from shore. In the course of the contact the two groups became so involved in doctrinal discussions that the leader of the refugees, Herman Backereel, requested a discussion with Menno Simons. This discussion was held on December 26, 1553. Feeling the need of support, the Reformed group summoned to their aid Martin Micron of Norden in East Friesland, one of their leading ministers. Micron and Menno held two lengthy discussions in the presence of many interested friends, both of them being held in the house where Menno lived. The dates of the two meetings were February 6 and 15, 1554. All three discussions, the two with Micron and the one with Backereel, were held in strict secrecy with a pledge by the Reformed group not to reveal Menno's hiding place to the magistrates. The meeting of February 6 dealt with the topics of baptism, the incarnation, oath, divorce, calling of ministers, functions of the civil authorities. It concluded peacefully. The second meeting, by request of Micron who knew Menno's weakness, was confined exclusively to the question of the incarnation and ended with bitterness on both sides. No account of these meetings was published until 1556 when Micron published a book under the title, *A True Account,* which contained a partial and somewhat inaccurate account of the proceedings including charges of a personal nature against Menno. Menno replied promptly in 1556 with *A Very Plain and Pointed Reply,* containing about two hundred pages, one of his longest writings. Two years later, in 1558, Micron returned to the fray with a book entitled, *A Reckoning.*

Soon after the discussion with Micron in 1554, Menno took part in another important meeting in Wismar of a quite different character, a conference of bishops and leaders of the Mennonite Church. Various matters of discipline had been creating difficulties, so that a meeting of the bishops had become necessary to secure and maintain unity and harmony in the church. The outcome of the conference was a set of nine resolutions dealing with such topics as marriage with nonmembers of the church, application of the ban, use of the courts of justice, the bearing and use of arms, and the necessity of a commission from the church and the bishop in order to preach. Unfortunately the text in which the resolutions have been preserved is so corrupt that it is impossible to be sure of the original meaning. Seven bishops took part in the meeting, Menno Simons being the leader. Among the others were Dirk Philips, Leonard Bouwens, and Gillis of Aachen. In respect to the exercise of the ban the resolutions took a rather strict position, so strict at least, that a conference of Swiss and South German brethren at Strasbourg in 1557 felt it necessary to pass a resolution disagreeing with the Wismar resolutions, and sent two delegates to Menno Simons to ask him to moderate the position on the ban taken by the North German bishops.

The increasing pressure of the civil and ecclesiastical authorities in Wismar against the Mennonites finally made it desirable for Menno Simons to leave the city. He therefore changed his residence during the spring or summer of 1554 to a location some distance westward near the town of Oldesloe between Lübeck and Hamburg. A certain nobleman by the name of Bartholomew von Ahlefeldt who lived in this vicinity had permitted Mennonite refugees fleeing from persecution elsewhere to settle upon his estate called "Fresenburg" as early as 1543. A Mennonite printer of Lübeck, who had operated a secret press on which he printed a large number of Mennonite books as well as many Bibles and concordances which were distributed as far west as Amsterdam, was compelled to seek a safer place for his operations. He moved first to Oldesloe, where ten casks full of books were confiscated, and finally to Fresenburg. He must have reached the latter place sometime during the latter part of 1554. Although it has not been definitely proved, it is altogether possible that the printer was Menno's printer, or even Menno himself, and that Menno accordingly had gone from Wismar to Lübeck, thence to Oldesloe, and finally to Fresenburg. It is more likely however that the printer was a well-to-do member of the church and a friend of Menno, since it is well known that Menno remained a poor man to the end of his life. At this time then Menno settled permanently at Wüstenfelde, a village on the estate of Fresenburg.

As persecution increased in the neighboring regions, more and more Mennonites found a haven of refuge under the protection of Baron von Ahlefeldt at Fresenburg and Wüstenfelde. The King of Denmark tried to persuade von Ahlefeldt to change his policy of toleration and drive the Brethren away, but he refused to do so, for he had been deeply and favorably impressed in his younger days by the steadfastness of the Mennonites under persecution, suffering, and death. Here in Fresenburg and Wüstenfelde Menno had time and peace to revise many of his earlier writings and to translate them from the original Dutch into the dialect spoken in this region which is called the "Oostersche" or eastern dialect. All his new writings written after 1554 were written in this dialect. A total of at least ten books and pamphlets were printed at Lübeck and Fresenburg during the years 1554-1561.

The last years of Menno's life were saddened by serious and at times bitter controversy among the churches of the west over matters of discipline, chiefly over the question of strictness in the matter of application of the ban and shunning of excommunicated members. As early as 1550, in his booklet on *Excommunication,* Menno had expressed the desire to be spared further trouble over this matter. The more serious divisions occurred after Menno's death.

The first news of the sharpened controversy over the ban reached Menno in 1555 in the form of a letter from five brethren "of good repute" living in Franeker in West Friesland, who reported that some desired that the ban be not imposed without preliminary warning three times except in cases of gross sin. Menno defended this more moderate procedure over against those who demanded an immediate and sharp application of the ban without warning.

An allied question which made a great deal of trouble was the question of shunning or avoidance of excommunicated members, particularly when members of the same family were involved. As the controversy grew warmer, letter after letter was sent to Menno from Holland begging him to take sides in the matter. Leonard Bouwens supported the radicals in their extreme demands, and when he finally threatened to expel a married woman in Emden because she refused to shun her husband, Menno was forced to take a stand. In a letter dated Nov. 12, 1556, he protested vigorously against extreme views and practices. He made a trip from Holstein to West Friesland in the hope of promoting unity and harmony, but met with only partial success, for a division still seemed to threaten. He returned home to Wüstenfelde, heartsore and grieving over the sad state of affairs in the church which he loved with all his heart. His feelings are well expressed in a letter addressed to his brother-in-law Reyn Edes in 1558: "O my brother Reyn! If I could only be with you even a half day and tell you something of my sorrow, my grief and heartache, and of the heavy burden which I carry for the future of the church. . . . If the mighty God had not strengthened me in the past year, as He is now doing also, I would have lost my reason. There is nothing on earth that I love so much as the church; yet just in respect to her must I suffer this great sorrow."

LABORS IN HOLSTEIN

Menno's strict position on the ban was to make additional trouble for him with other groups of Mennonites in the Rhineland and in South Germany. In April, 1556, before he had gone to West Friesland, two brethren from the Rhineland, by name Zylis and Lemke, together with others, had visited him in Wüstenfelde to discuss the question of the ban and shunning. They were inclined to be less strict. They left Menno only partially convinced, but agreed to consider the matter further and lay it before certain South German brethren for counsel. Menno gave Zylis a written statement of his position to take along to show the South Germans.

When they finally reported Menno's views on the question of shunning to the very important conference in Strasbourg in 1557 at which over fifty bishops from many countries took part, they received a strongly negative reaction. The conference adopted a resolution rejecting the shunning of married partners and formulated a letter addressed to Menno and his fellow bishops in North Germany and Holland containing an earnest appeal for moderation in the matter of shunning. In the letter they expressed the strong desire to be one in peace and unity with the brethren in the North. They also indicated disagreement with Menno's peculiar theory of the incarnation.

The appeal of the Strasbourg conference was to be in vain. The unity was not reached, for the brethren in the North were implacable in the matter of shunning. In the year 1558 both Menno and Dirk Philips published strong tracts on the question. In Menno's tract, entitled *Of Excommunication,* the strict position on shunning which demanded that all human ties, including those of marriage and the family, must give way under the ban of

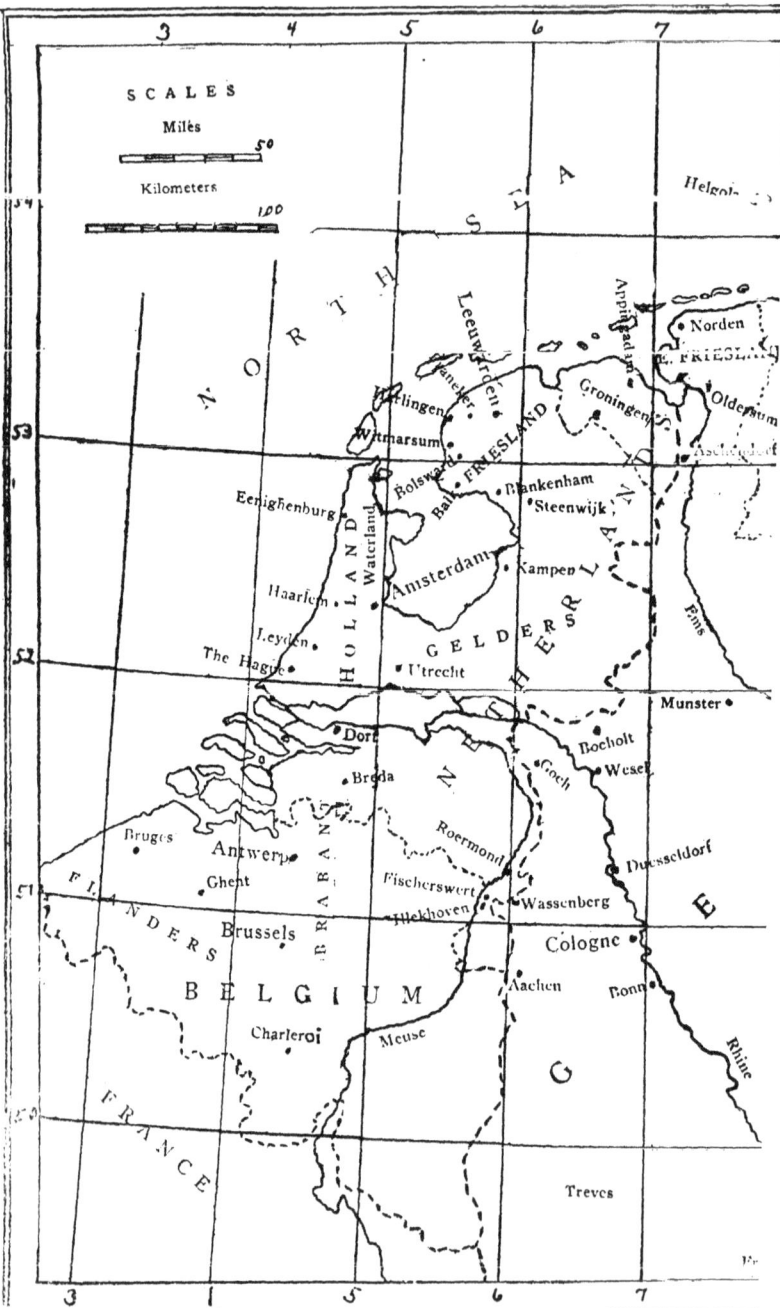

the church, was clearly taught. This pamphlet stirred up further controversy. Zylis and Lemke took the lead in opposing Menno, so that he felt it necessary to publish a tract against them on January, 1560, entitled *Reply to Zylis and Lemke*. In this pamphlet, which was his last writing, Menno defended himself, and finally announced that he could no longer regard the two men as brethren.

Menno's time after this episode was but short. His health had never been strong, and his life of hardships and privations, as well as the burden of the churches, undermined what health he had, particularly since he had been crippled in Wismar so that he had to use a crutch at times. His death came upon him on his sick bed January 31, 1561, just twenty-five years after his renunciation of Catholicism at Witmarsum. His wife had preceded him in death between 1553 and 1558, as well as two children, a daughter and a son. One daughter survived him. He was buried in his own garden in Wüstenfelde. Unfortunately the place can no longer be determined with accuracy because of the destruction of Wüstenfelde in the devastation of Fresenburg in the Thirty Years War. The plot of ground was located as nearly as possible in 1906 when a modest memorial was erected in memory of Menno's labors in the service of God and the church he loved.

CHAPTER VI

THE SIGNIFICANCE OF MENNO SIMONS

Menno Simons was not the founder of the Mennonite Church. The Mennonite Church was founded in Zurich, Switzerland in January, 1525 by Conrad Grebel, Felix Manz, George Blaurock, and others, eleven years before Menno Simons renounced Catholicism. Nor did Menno found the church in Holland. If any one deserves that title it was Obbe Philips who began to gather the brethren in Friesland about 1533. Yet there is good historical reason for the Mennonite Church to bear the name of Menno Simons, for in the time of greatest need Menno Simons was the heaven-sent leader who rallied the scattered brethren, and gave them the leadership in faith and spirit and doctrine which they needed. He it was who led them safely through the time of great tribulation "in spite of dungeon, fire, and sword."

Menno's greatness lay not so much in his eloquence, although he was a good preacher, nor in his literary craftsmanship, although he could write well for the common man. He was no great theologian, although he knew how to present the plain teachings of the Bible with force and clarity. He was not even a great organizer, although he rendered a real service in the guidance which he gave to the bishops and ministers of the growing church. Yet, Menno Simons was one of the great religious leaders of his day and land, perhaps the most outstanding religious leader of the Netherlands in his time. His work and influence have had permanent significance on the history of the people and church which bears his name, and through them his influence has reached the larger circles of the free churches of England and America.

The greatness of Menno Simons lies in three factors of influence, his character, his writings, and his message. His character was a steadying, heartening, building influence in the long, hard years of persecution and struggle from 1535 to 1560, with his deep conviction, unshakable devotion, fearless courage, and calm trust. His writings, though they seem at times, as gathered together in his complete works, to be repetitious and insignificant, included some admirable tracts for the times, pointed, plain, well-adapted to their purpose. They reached the common people at the right time, and were powerful agents in the building and strengthening of the church and in winning new adherents. But most of all it was the message of Menno Simons which made him a great leader in a great cause. He built no great system of theology, nor did he discover any great new or long-lost principle; he merely caught a clear vision of two fundamental Biblical ideals, the ideal of practical holiness, and the ideal of the high place of the church in the life of the believer and in the cause of Christ.

On the basis of the first ideal he called for a genuine change of life and the faithful practice of the Christian way of life as Christ taught and lived it, the life of righteousness, holiness, purity, love and peace. For him Christianity was more than faith only, it was faith and works. And this practical Christianity meant for Menno the resolute abandonment by the Christian of all carnal strife and war, indeed of the use of force in any manner, as well as a thoroughgoing separation from the sin of the worldly social order. The ideal of the Church which Menno held was the organizing principle of Christian doctrine and life in his entire thinking. For him the Church was the representative and agent of Christ on earth, and as such was to keep itself holy and pure in life and doctrine, and was to give a faithful witness for Christ until He came. These ideals of Menno have been the major formative ideals throughout the four hundred years of Mennonite history, for they were shared by the Swiss-South German Mennonites as well. They constitute the genius of the Mennonite Church. Out of them was born the ideal of complete separation of church and state, of toleration and freedom of conscience, of high moral and social ideals, of the preaching and practice of peace, of the supreme sovereignty of Christ over His own in this worldly world of ours,—all ideals far in advance of their day, but which today have fairly become the common and cherished possession of a large section of English and American Protestantism.

It is, therefore not for the greatness of Menno Simons, the man, and his human achievements, that we bring this tribute,—the tribute we bring is to the greatness of the ideals and convictions which possessed his soul and commanded his life, and which have blessed countless thousands since his day.

EXCERPTS FROM MENNO SIMONS' WRITINGS ON CHRISTIAN DOCTRINE

1. *The Authority of the Scriptures*

Dear reader, I admonish and advise you, if you seek God with all your heart and would not be deceived, do not depend upon men and the doctrine of men, however old, holy and excellent it may be esteemed, for one theologian is against the other, both in ancient and modern times; but build upon Christ and His Word alone, upon the sure teaching and practice of His holy apostles, and you will through the grace of God be kept safe from all false doctrine and from the power of the devil, and walk before your God with a confident and pious mind. (I:37).

This holy Christian church has only one doctrine—the pure, unmixed and unadulterated Word of God, the Gospel of grace of our Lord Jesus Christ. All teachings and decrees that do not accord with the doctrine of Christ, be they the teachings and opinions of doctors, decrees of popes, ecumenical councils, or anything else, are but teachings and commandments of men (Matt. 19:5), doctrines of devils (I Tim. 4:1) and therefore accursed (Gal. 7:8). We write and teach nothing but the pure, heavenly Word and the perfect commandments of Jesus Christ and His apostles. (II:193b).

But that he appeals to Tertullian, Cyprian, Origen and Augustine, my reply is, first, If these writers can support their teaching with the Word and command of God, we will admit that they are right. If not, then it is a doctrine of men and accursed according to the Scriptures. Gal. 1:8. (II:49a).

We tell you the truth and lie not. If any one under the canopy of heaven can show us from Scripture that Jesus Christ, the Son of the Almighty God, the eternal wisdom and truth, whom alone we acknowledge as the lawgiver and teacher of the New Testament, has commanded one word to that effect, or that His holy apostles have ever taught or practiced the like, there is no need of an attempt to compel us by tyranny and torture. Only show us God's Word and the question is settled. (I:31a).

Therefore I deem it needful and well, sincerely to warn and admonish my beloved readers, not to accept my doctrine as the Gospel of Jesus Christ until they have investigated for themselves and found it to agree with the Spirit and Word of the Lord, that their faith may not be founded on me nor on any other teacher or writer, but solely on Jesus Christ. (II:248b).

2. *The Trinity of God*

We believe and confess with the Holy Scriptures that there is an only, eternal God who created heaven and earth, the sea and all that therein is; a God whom heaven and the heaven of heavens can not comprehend; whose throne is heaven, and the earth is His footstool; a God of gods and a Lord of lords, who is above all, mighty, holy, terrible, praiseworthy and wonderful; a consuming fire; whose kingdom, power, dominion, majesty and glory is eternal, and shall endure forever. . . . And since He is a Spirit so great and awe-inspiring, and invisible, He is also inexpressible, incomprehensible, indescribable. (II: 183).

This only, eternal, omnipotent, ineffable, invisible, inexpressible and indescribable God we believe and confess with the Scriptures to be the eternal, incomprehensible Father, with His eternal, incomprehensible Son, and with His eternal, incomprehensible Holy Spirit. The Father we confess to be truly Father: the Son truly Son and the Holy Spirit truly Holy Spirit, not carnal and comprehensible but spiritual and incomprehensible, for Christ says: "God is a Spirit." (II:183).

John says: "There are three that bear record in heaven, the Father, the Word and the Holy Ghost, and these three are one." Read also Matt. 28:19; Mark 1:8; Luke 3:8; John 14:16; 15:26; I Cor. 12:11. And although they are three, yet in divinity, will, power and working they are one and can no more be separated from each other, than the sun, brightness and warmth, for the one is not without the other. (II:187).

My dear brethren, I for myself confess that I would rather die than to believe and teach to my brethren a single word concerning the Father, the Son and the Holy Ghost, at variance with the express testimony of God's Word, as it is so clearly given through the mouth of the prophets, evangelists and apostles. (II:188b).

3. *Christ, His Deity and Humanity*

We teach and believe that Jesus Christ is God's first and only begotten Son, the incomprehensible, eternal Word, by whom all things are created, the first-born of every creature, Col. 1:15; that He became a true man in Mary, the immaculate virgin, through the almighty, eternal Father's eternal Spirit and power, beyond the comprehension and knowledge of men; sent and given unto us out of pure mercy and grace, from the Father; the express image of the invisible God and the brightness of His glory, Heb. 1:3. (I:113).

And the incomprehensible, inexpressible, spiritual, eternal divine Being which is divinely and incomprehensibly begotten of the Father, before every creature, we believe and confess to be Jesus Christ, the first and only begotten Son of God, "the first-born of every creature," the eternal wisdom, the power of God, the eternal light, truth and life, the eternal Word.

Beloved brethren, understand me rightly, I say eternal wisdom, eternal power. For, as we believe and confess that the Father was from eternity and will eternally remain, yea, that He is the First and the Last, so we also freely believe and confess that His wisdom, His power, His light, His truth, His life, His Word, Jesus Christ, has from eternity been with Him and in Him, yea that He is the Alpha and Omega, or else we should have to confess that this begotten, incomprehensible truly divine Being, Christ Jesus, whom the church fathers called a person, through whom the eternal Father has made all things, has had a beginning like a creature; an opinion which all true Christians look upon as a terrible curse, blasphemy, and abomination. (II:184).

That He had the true human nature, as well as the divine, He has shown by the apparent evidence of the real human nature, as by hungering, thirsting, being weary, sighing, weariness, suffering and death. (II:392).

Behold, faithful brethren, here you have the incomprehensible birth of Christ, His divine glory, working and power, and numerous precious and plain testimonies of the holy prophets, evangelists and apostles, all of whom with invincible power and clearness testify and point out the true, incomprehensible divinity of our Lord Jesus Christ. (II:186b).

We believe and confess Christ Jesus with His heavenly Father to be truly God; and that because of the plain testimony of the holy prophets, evangelists and apostles. (II:186a).

I say that concerning this incomprehensible, sublime subject I do in no wise make reason my counselor, but set forth the word of my Lord which teaches me in all clearness, etc. (II:398a). Although He humbled Himself and for our sakes for a time laid down His divine privilege, right and majesty, notwithstanding this He was God and God's Word (II:164a). Christ is truly God and man, man and God (II:330b; also II:153b). I confess both natures in Christ, the divine and the human. (II:375b).

4. *The Incarnation*

Faithful reader, observe: just as I do not comprehend the almighty, only and eternal God in His divine nature, in the dominion of His glory, in the creation and preservation of His creatures, in the recompensation of both the good and the evil, and in many of His works, yet I do truly believe in Him as such, and for this reason: because the Scripture teaches it, so likewise I can not comprehend how, or in what manner the incomprehensible, eternal Word became flesh, or man, in Mary. Nevertheless, I do truly believe that He became man because the Scripture teaches it. (II:160b).

Inasmuch as we clearly find and know that the Holy Ghost has not revealed this mystery [of the Incarnation] in the Scriptures that He has not revealed it unto us in any manner, neither by any prophet, nor apostle, nor by the Son Himself, and inasmuch as it is manifest that it can not be fathomed by reason . . . and besides we learn from history and find in our own time that many sharp eyes have been blinded by this impenetrable brightness, therefore I warn all pious hearts that would walk with a clear conscience before their God, not to speculate about this ineffable and indescribable majesty of the incomprehensible eternal Godhead, and not to conclude, assert, teach, or maintain above that which the Holy Spirit has revealed and taught us in His Holy Word. (II:369).

And therefore I say that I do not at all undertake to reason out this incomprehensible point, but will follow the word of my Lord which is quite clear in this instance. (II: 398a).

5. *The Holy Spirit*

As we have now pointed out and confessed our faith and doctrine of the true divinity of Christ, we will also now, by the grace of God, set forth in few words our faith and confession of the Holy Ghost. Let the God-fearing judge. We believe and confess the Holy Ghost to be a true, real, or personal Holy Ghost, and this in a divine sense — even as the Father is truly Father and the Son truly Son; which Holy Ghost is [in His nature] incomprehensible, inexpressible and indescribable, as we have also testified of the Father and the Son. He is divine in His attributes, proceeding from the Father through the Son, although He ever remains with God and in God and is never separated in His nature from the Father and the Son. And the reason why we confess Him to be such a true and personal Holy Spirit is, because we are impelled to it by the Scriptures. (II:186b).

He guides us into all truth; He justifies us; He cleanses, sanctifies, pacifies, consoles, reproves, cheers and assures us; He testifies to our spirit that we are the children of God. — Yea, my brethren, from these plain Scriptures, testimonies and references and a great many other texts which are too lengthy to quote, and which may be found in the Scriptures and read, we believe the Holy Ghost to be the true Spirit of God who adorns us with His heavenly and divine gifts, frees us from sin, makes us cheerful, peaceful, pious, satisfies our hearts and minds and makes us holy in Christ Jesus. (II:187a).

6. Sin

Just as Adam and Eve were bitten and poisoned by the infernal serpent, and became sinful by nature and would have been subject to eternal death, if God had not through Jesus Christ again accepted them in grace [after they had made the promise Gen. 3:15 their own], as stated above, so also all we who are their descendants are by birth of a sinful nature, are poisoned by the serpent, inclined toward evil and thus by our own inherent nature are children of hell, etc. We cannot be saved therefrom (we speak of those who have come to the years of understanding and have committed sins) unless we, by true and unfeigned faith, accept Christ Jesus, the only and eternal means of grace, and thus with the eyes of our mind look upon the brazen serpent, which for us miserable, poisoned sinners, is lifted up by God our heavenly Father, as a sign of salvation; for apart from Him and without Him there is no salvation for our souls, no atonement nor peace, but only disgrace, wrath and death is to be looked for eternally. (II:261b).

Wherever these two, namely original sin—the mother—and actual sins—the fruits—are in evidence and in power, there is no forgiveness nor promise of life, but there abide wrath and death, unless they are repented of, as the Scriptures teach. If this inherent sin is to lose its strength in us and actual sin be forgiven, we must believe the word of the Lord, be born again by faith, and in the strength of this new birth, through true repentance, resist the inherent sin, die unto actual sin and be spiritually minded. (II:313a).

I did not know my condition as long as it was not pointed out to me by Thy Spirit. I thought I was a Christian, but when I proved myself rightly, I realized that I was quite earthly, carnal and without Thy Word.—O dear Lord, I knew myself not till I viewed myself in Thy Word; then I learned to know with Paul my blindness, nakedness, uncleanness, depraved nature, and that nothing good dwelt in my flesh. (I:217b).

7. *The Atonement*

I think this may well be called a joyous Gospel and glad tidings to all convicted and troubled souls who, through the law, have been brought to a knowledge of their sin and know that they are in danger of eternal death, who tremble before the righteous judgment and wrath of God—that the almighty, eternal God and Father has so loved us poor, perishing sinners who were so far estranged from Him and according to His righteous judgment had deserved eternal death, that He sent into this world His almighty, eternal Word, His only, eternal and beloved Son, the brightness of His glory, as a poor mortal man, like unto Adam before the fall, as a proof and means of His grace; and that He through His perfect righteousness, willing obedience and innocent death, has brought us from the kingdom and dominion of Satan into the kingdom of His divine grace and eternal peace. (II: 167a).

There will in eternity be found no other remedy for our sins, neither in heaven nor upon earth, neither works, merits nor ordinances (even though they are observed according to the Scriptures), neither persecution nor tribulation, neither the innocent blood of the saints, nor angels, nor men, nor any other means, but alone the immaculate blood of the Lamb which out of pure grace, mercy and love was shed once for all for the remission of our sins. (I:155b).

They all seek some remedy for their sins, but the only true remedy, Christ, they do not recognize; they have therefore contrived so many remedies that we can neither describe nor relate them all, such as the Romish indulgences, holy water, fastings, confessions, masses, pilgrimages, infant baptism, bread and wine, etc. (I: 51a).

My dear reader, the truth we testify to you in Christ; you may believe, do, hope and seek where and what you choose, we are assured that you will in eternity find no other remedy for your sins which will avail before God, than the one we have pointed out to you, which is Jesus

Christ, else all Scripture must be erroneous and false. (I:51b).

All those, therefore, that seek other remedies for their sins, however great and holy they may appear, than the remedy provided by God alone, deny the Lord's death, which He suffered for us, and His innocent blood which He shed for us. (I:52a).

There is no remedy against sin besides the precious blood of Jesus Christ; neither works nor merits, neither baptism nor supper (although I know well that the true Christians use these signs in obedience to the divine word); otherwise that which we obtain through the merits of Christ is ascribed and given to elements and creatures. The Christian ordinances are signs of obedience through which our faith is exercised.—We find that the new birth is brought about through God's Word (Rom. 10:14; I Cor. 4:15; Jas. 1:18; I Pet. 1:23).

8. *Repentance*

Behold, dear reader, such repentance we teach, namely to die to the old sinful life and to live no longer according to the lusts of the flesh, but do as David did. When he was reproved by the prophet for his sin, he wept bitterly, cried to God, forsook evil and committed such sinful abominations no more. Peter sinned very grievously once and no more. Matthew, after his call, did not return into his old life. Zaccheus and the sinful woman did not again become guilty of the impure works of darkness. Zaccheus made restitution to those whom he had overcharged and defrauded and gave half his goods to the poor and distressed. The woman wept very bitterly and washed the feet of the Lord with her tears; she anointed them with precious ointment and sat humbly at His feet to listen to His blessed words. These are the true fruits of that repentance which is acceptable to the Lord. (I: 18a).

Such repentance we teach, and no other, namely that no one may rightfully glory in God's grace, forgiveness of his sin and the merits of Christ, unless the fruits of true repentance are found in his life. It is not enough that we say, We are Abraham's children, that is that we bear the Christian name, but we must have the works of Abraham (John 8:39). We must walk as all true children of God are bidden and commanded in the Word of the Lord; as John says: "If we say that we have fellowship with him, and walk in darkness, we lie, and the truth is not in us. But if we walk in the light as he is in the light, we have fellowship one with another, and the blood of Jesus Christ his Son cleanseth us from all sin" (I John 1:6, 7). (I: 18b).

But if you would rightly confess and repent, and receive true absolution of God, approach Him with a believing, penitent, contrite heart, with a sorrowing, distressed mind, forsake sin, do justly and right to your neighbor, love, help, serve, reprove and comfort him, as you ought. And if you have sinned against him or in any way taken unfair advantage of him, confess it to him and satisfy him. Behold this is the only true Auricular Confession and penance taught in the Word of God. (I: 148a).

9. *Faith*

True faith which avails before God, is a living and saving power which is, through the preaching of the holy word, bestowed of God on the heart, moving, changing and regenerating it to newness of mind. It destroys all ungodliness, all pride, unholy ambition and selfishness, makes us children in malice, etc. Behold, such is the faith which the Scriptures teach us, and not a vain, dead, and unfruitful illusion, as the world dreams. (II:59a).

Yes, dear reader, true Christian faith as it is required in Scripture, is so living, active and strong in all those who through the grace of the Lord have rightly obtained it, that they do not hesitate to forsake father, mother, wife, children, money and possessions for the Word and testimony of the Lord; to suffer all manner of scorn, disgrace, hardship and prison, and finally to have their weak bodies burned at the stake, as may be frequently seen in many pious children of God and faithful witnesses for Christ especially in these our Netherlands. (I:158a).

Since then faith so fully realizes that God can not break His promise, but must keep it, because He is the truth and can not lie, as was said, therefore faith makes the believers frankhearted, joyous and cheerful in the Spirit, though they be confined in prisons and bonds, or suffer death by water, fire or the sword. For they are assured in the spirit through faith that God can not break His promise toward them, but will fulfill it in due time. They believe in Christ in whom the promise has been sealed, they recognize through Him also His grace, word and will, notwithstanding that in former times they lived so ungodly and walked according to the flesh. (I:159a).

Not, dear reader, that we believe that faith merits this on account of its own worth; by no means; but the pleasure of God has attached His promise to true, genuine faith through the Word. Faith saves, not through its own worth or merit, but through the promise which is attached to it. (I:159a).

Observe here that true Christian faith through grace is the only fountain whence flows not only the contrite new life but also obedience as concerns the evangelical ceremonies, such as baptism and the Lord's Supper, not as compelled by law, for the rod of the oppressor is broken, but through the voluntary, submissive spirit of love which by virtue of its Christ-like nature is willing and ready for every good work in obedience to the holy divine Word. (I:158a).

10. *Justification by Faith*

Those who trust in their works or ceremonies for salvation deny thereby the grace and merits of Christ. For if our reconciliation consisted in works and ceremonies, grace would come to naught and the merits and virtue of the blood of Christ would all be void. O no! it is grace and will be grace in all eternity, all that the merciful Father through His dear Son and Holy Spirit has done for us grievous sinners. (I:158a).

But that we avoid sinful works and desire to conform ourselves in our weakness to His word and command, this we do because He has thus taught and commanded us. For whosoever does not walk according to His doctrine, testifies by his deeds that he does not believe in Him nor know Him, and that he is not in the communion of the saints. (John 15:7; I John 3:10; 5:10; II John 6). (II:262).

We teach emphatically that by no outward works, however great and good they may appear, we could be saved or entirely please God, for they all are in every instance mixed with imperfection and weakness, and through them, on account of the corruption of the flesh, we can not acquire the righteousness required in the commandments. We point therefore alone to Jesus Christ who is our only and eternal righteousness, reconciliation and propitiation with the Father, and know of no trust in our own works. My reader, I write the truth in Christ and lie not. (II:25a).

Mark, beloved reader, we do not believe nor teach that salvation is of our merits and works, as our opponents accuse us without any truth, but solely by grace, through Christ Jesus, as has been said. (II:263a).

11. *Regeneration*

The new birth consists verily not in water nor in words, but it is the heavenly quickening power of God in our hearts which comes from God and through the preaching of the divine word, if we accept the same by faith, touches, pierces, renews and changes our hearts, so that we are converted from unbelief to faith, from unrighteousness to righteousness, from evil to good, from carnality to spirituality, from the earthly to the heavenly, from the evil nature of Adam to the good nature of Jesus Christ. (II:215a).

All who accept by faith this grace in Christ which is preached through the Gospel, and adhere to it from their hearts, are born anew of God, through the power of the Holy Ghost. Their heart and mind is changed and renewed; yea, they are transferred from Adam into Christ. They walk in newness of life, as willing and obedient children, in the grace that is extended to them. They are renewed, I say, have become poor in spirit, meek, merciful, compassionate, peaceable, patient, hungry and thirsty after righteousness, ready to suffer for the truth; they strive steadfastly by good works after eternal life; for they are believing, they are born of God, they are in Christ and Christ in them; they partake of His Spirit and nature and thus live by the power of Christ which is in them, according to the Word of the Lord. This is what it means, according to the Scriptures to believe, to be Christians, to be in Christ and Christ in us. (I:147b).

God does not seek words nor appearance but power and deed. Do you think it sufficient if you know Christ only according to the flesh? Or if you but say that you believe on Him, that you are baptized and are Christians, and that you are purchased by the blood and death of Christ? Ah no! I have told you often and tell you again, you must be born of God and your life changed and converted in such a manner that you are new men in Christ, that Christ be in you and you in Christ, or you can never be Christians, for, If any man be in Christ, he is a new creature. (I:172b).

But, first and above all, if you would be saved, your earthly, carnal, ungodly life must be changed. For all the Scriptures, with all their admonitions, threatening, reproving, miracles, examples, ceremonies and ordinances teach us nothing but repentance and a new life. And if you do not repent, there is nothing in heaven or on earth that can help you, for without true repentance one is comforted in vain. We must be born from above, must be changed and renewed in our hearts and thus be transplanted from the unrighteous and evil nature of Adam into the righteous and good nature of Christ, or we can not be helped in eternity by any means, whether divine or human.

The regeneration of which we write, from which follows the contrite, pious life having the promise, comes alone from the Word of the Lord if it is rightly taught and is through the Holy Spirit rightly received into the heart through faith. (I:169a).

12. *Holiness of Life*

For true evangelical faith is of such nature that it can not be workless or idle; it ever manifests its powers. For as it is the nature of fire to produce nothing but heat and flame, of the sun nothing but light and heat, the water moisture, and a good tree good fruit after its natural properties, so also true evangelical faith brings forth true evangelical fruit, in accordance with its true, good, evangelical nature. (I:118b).

The true believers show in act and deed that they believe, are born of God and spiritually minded. They lead a pious, unblameable life before all men, they are baptized according to the Lord's command, as a proof and testimony that their sins are taken away through Christ's death and that they desire to walk with Him in newness of life; they break the bread of peace with their beloved brethren, as a proof and testimony that they are one with Christ and with His church and that they have or know no other means of grace and of remission of their sins, neither in heaven nor upon earth, than the innocent body and blood of our Lord Jesus Christ alone, which He once through His eternal Spirit, in obedience to the Father, has offered up and shed upon the cross for us poor sinners. They walk in all love and mercy, they serve their neighbors, etc. In short, they order their lives, in their weakness, according to all the words, commandments, ordinances, spirit, rule, example and measure of Christ, as the Scriptures teach; for they are in Christ and Christ is in them. And therefore they live no longer in the old life of sin after the first earthly Adam (weakness excepted), but in the new life of righteousness which is by faith, after the second and heavenly Adam, Christ; as Paul says, "I do not now live, but Christ liveth in me, and the life which I now live in the flesh, I live by the faith of the Son of God who loved me, and gave himself for me" (Gal. 2:20). And Christ says, that those who love Him will keep His commandments. (John 14:15). (II: 262b).

Besides we teach the true love and fear of God, the true love of our neighbor, to serve and aid all mankind and to injure none, to crucify the flesh and its desires and lusts, to prune the heart, mouth and the whole body with the knife of the divine word, of all unclean thoughts, unbecoming words and actions. Consider now whether this is not the will of God, the true doctrine of Jesus Christ, the rightful use of the ordinances, and the true life, which is of God, although all the gates of hell may willfully oppose it. (II:244a).

Again the thoughts of those who are Christians in fact are pure and chaste, their words are true and seasoned with salt; with them yea is yea and nay nay, and their works are done in the fear of the Lord. Their hearts are heavenly and renewed, their minds peaceful and joyous; they seek righteousness with all their heart. In short, they have through the Spirit and word of God such assurance of their faith, that they will through such faith valiantly overcome all bloodthirsty, cruel tyrants with all their tortures, imprisonments, exiling, spoiling of their property, stocks, stakes, executioners, tormentors and henchmen; and out of a godly zeal, with an innocent, pure heart, with simple yea and nay they are willing to die. The glory of Christ, the sweetness of the Word and the salvation of their souls are dearer to them than all that is under heaven. (I:170a).

13. *The Church*

The true messengers of the Gospel who are one with Christ in spirit, love and life, teach that which is entrusted to them by Christ, namely repentance and the peaceable Gospel of grace which He Himself has received of the Father and taught the world. All who hear, believe, accept and rightly fulfill the same are the church of Christ, the true, believing Christian church, the body and bride of Christ, the ark of the Lord, etc. They are chosen to proclaim the power of Him who has called them from darkness unto His marvelous light. (II:345b).

Christ's church consists of the chosen of God, His saints and beloved who have washed their robes in the blood of the Lamb, who are born of God and led by Christ's Spirit, who are in Christ and Christ in them, who hear and believe His word, live in their weakness according to His commandments and in patience and meekness follow in His footsteps, who hate evil and love the good, earnestly desiring to apprehend Christ as they are apprehended of Him. For all who are in Christ are new creatures, flesh of His flesh, bone of His bone and members of His body. (I:161b).

The true characteristics by which the Church of Christ may be known:
1. The unadulterated pure doctrine.
2. The scriptural use of the ordinances.
3. Obedience to the Word.
4. Unfeigned brotherly love.
5. Candid confession of God and Christ.
6. Bearing oppression and hatred for the sake of the Word of the Lord. (II:83b).

Some of the other parables, as of the net in which good and bad fishes are caught; of the wise and foolish virgins and their lamps; of the wedding of the king's son and the guests, and of the threshing floor with wheat and chaff, although the Lord spoke them in allusion to the church, yet they were not spoken for the purpose that the church should knowingly and willfully accept and suffer open transgressors in its communion; because in that case Christ and Paul would differ in doctrine, for Paul says that such should be disciplined and avoided. But they were spoken because many intermingle with the Christians in a Christian semblance, and place themselves under the Word and its sacraments who in fact are no Christians, but are hypocrites and dissemblers before their God; and these are likened unto the refuse fish which will be cast out by the angels at the day of Christ; unto the foolish virgins who had no oil in their lamps; unto the guest without a wedding garment and unto the chaff. For they pretend that they fear God and seek Christ; they receive baptism and the Lord's Supper and outwardly have a good appearance, but do not have faith, repentance, true fear and love of God, Spirit, power, fruit, works and deeds. (II:88b).

14. *Called out From the World*

The whole evangelical Scriptures teach that Christ's church was and must be a people separated from the world in doctrine, life and worship. It was likewise in the Old Testament (II Cor. 6:17; Tit. 2:14; I Pet. 2:9, 10; I Cor. 5:17; Ex. 19:12).

Since the church always was and must be a separated people, as has been heard, and it is clear as the meridian sun that for many centuries no difference has been observable between the church and the world, but all people have been blended together in baptism, supper, life and worship without any separation, a condition which is so clearly contrary to all Scripture, therefore we are constrained by the Spirit and word of God to the praise of Christ and to the service and betterment of our neighbor from true motives, as set forth above, to gather not to us but to the Lord, a pious, penitent assembly or church . . . not by force of arms or uproar (as is the custom of the popular sects), a church which is separated from the world, as the Scriptures teach. (II:38a).

The ministers [of the state churches] should preach rightly the word of sincere repentance in the power of the Spirit. All those who accept it with a believing heart and truly repent, should then be served with Christ's sacraments according to divine institution. And those who would wickedly, deliberately despise it, should in the power of the holy word be separated from the communion of their church, without respect of persons, be they rich or poor. In this way they could begin to gather a church unto Christ and in it rightly practice the ordinances of the Lord according to the Scriptures. (II:70).

15. *A True Brotherhood*

In the fourth place some of them charge and assert that we have our property in common. We reply that this charge is false and altogether without foundation. We do not teach nor practice the doctrine of having all property in common. But we teach and maintain by the word of the Lord that all true believers are members of one body, are baptized by one Spirit into one body (I Cor. 10:18) and have one Lord and one God (Eph. 4:5, 6).

Inasmuch as they are thus one, therefore it is Christian and reasonable that they truly love one another and that the one member be solicitous for the welfare of the other, for both the Scriptures and nature teach it. All Scripture urges charity and love, and it is the one sign by which a true Christian may be known, as the Lord says, "By this shall all men know that ye are my disciples (that is, that ye are Christians) if ye have love one to another" (John 13:35).

Beloved reader, it has not been heard of that an intelligent person clothes and cares for one part of his body and leaves the rest destitute and naked. O no, it is but natural to care for all the members. Thus it must be with those who are the Lord's church or body. All who are born of God, are partakers of the Spirit of the Lord and are called into one body of love, according to the Scriptures, are ready by such love to serve their neighbors, not only with money and goods, but also, according to the example of their Lord and Head, Jesus Christ, in an evangelical manner, with life and blood.

They practice charity and love as much as they have ability; they suffer no one to be a beggar among them; they distribute to the necessity of the saints, receive the miserable, take the stranger into their houses, console the afflicted, assist the needy, cloth the naked, feed the hungry, do not turn their face from the poor, and do not despise their own suffering members — their own flesh. Isa. 58: 7, 8. (II:309a).

To repeat: This love, charity and community we teach and practice, and have for seventeen years taught and practiced in such manner that although we have to a great extent been robbed of our property and are yet robbed, and many a pious, God-fearing father and mother has been put to death by the fire, water, or the sword, and we have no secure place of abode, as is manifest, and besides there are dear times, yet, thanks be to God, none of the pious, nor any of their children who have been committed to us, have been found to beg. (II:309b).

They boast of following the word of God, and of being the true Christian church, and never realize that they have entirely lost the evidence of true Christianity. For although they have plenty of everything and many of their own people fare sumptuously and live in voluptuousness, in superfluous expense, going about in silk and velvet, gold and silver and all kinds of pomp and pride and furnish their houses with all manner of costly ornaments, and have their coffers well filled, yet they suffer many of their poor afflicted members, although they are their fellow believers, have received one baptism and partaken of the same bread with them, to go begging, some of them suffering from the bitterest want, hunger and need, and so many of their aged, sick, lame, blind members are compelled to beg their bread at their doors. (II:310a).

16. *The Ordinances*

For the truly regenerated and spiritually minded conform in all things to the word and ordinances of the Lord; not for the reason that they suppose to merit the propitiation of their sins and eternal life; by no means. For this they depend on nothing except the blood and merits of Christ, relying upon the sure promise of the merciful Father which was graciously given to all believers, which blood alone, I say again, is and ever will be the only and eternally valid means of our reconciliation, and not works, baptism or Lord's Supper, as said above. (I:158a).

Repentance must come before the ordinances, and not the ordinances before repentance. For the ordinances of the New Testament are in themselves quite powerless, vain and useless, if that which they signify, namely the new contrite life is not in evidence as has been said above in treating of baptism. (II:65a).

This is briefly, in all matters that concern the Christian church, my only foundation and sincere conviction, that before God neither baptism, nor the Supper, nor any other outward ordinances avail if partaken without the Spirit of God and the new creature, but that before God only faith, spirit, the new creature or regeneration avail, as Paul plainly teaches, Gal. 5:6. All who by the grace of God have received these from above, will be baptized according to the command of the Lord and rightly partake of the Supper. Yea, with ardent desire they accept all the ordinances and doctrine of Jesus Christ and shall never willfully oppose the holy will and plain testimony of God. (II:349b).

Ceremonies without the reality are not valid before God. For He is not such a God who has pleasure in any outward shadow, ceremony, type, bread, wine, water, and nominal service, but in spirit, power, deed and truth.

Again, the prince of darkness, the old serpent and the devil, can transform himself into an angel of light. Nothing of an external nature is oppressive or vexatious to him; if he can only gain possession of the citadel of our hearts, and expel therefrom Christ's nature, spirit and power, he has already won the price of his craftiness. Yea, if a man were baptized even by Peter or Paul himself, and received the bread of the holy Supper from the Lord's own hand, and never again witnessed the idolatry of the priests, yet if he retained but one of the fruits of the devil whether hatred, envy or bitterness, revengefulness or avarice, pride or unchastity, or any other vice, it would have to be said with the Scriptures that his spirit is ungodly and his life hypocrisy. (I:265a).

17. *Baptism*

We are not regenerated because we have been baptized, . . . but we are baptized because we have been regenerated by faith and the Word of God (I Pet. 1:23). Regeneration is not the result of baptism, but baptism the result of regeneration. This can indeed not be controverted by any man, or disproved by the Scriptures. (II:215a).

The Scriptures know of only one remedy, which is Christ with His merits, death and blood. Hence, he who seeks the remission of his sins through baptism, rejects the blood of the Lord and makes water his idol. Therefore let every one have a care, lest he ascribe the honor and glory due to Christ, to the outward ceremonies and visible elements. (I:32a).

The believing receive remission of sins not through baptism, but in baptism, in the following manner: as with their whole heart they believe the precious Gospel of Jesus Christ which has been preached and taught to them, namely the glad tidings of grace, remission of sins, peace, favor, mercy and eternal life through Jesus Christ, our Lord, they experience a change of mind, renounce self, bitterly repent of their old sinful life, and with all diligence give attendance to the Word of the Lord who has shown them such great love; and fulfill all that He has taught and commanded in His holy Gospel. Their confidence is firmly established upon the word of grace promising the remission of sins through the precious blood and the merits of our Lord Jesus Christ. They therefore receive holy baptism as a token of obedience which proceeds from faith, an evidence before God and His church that they firmly believe in the remission of sins through Christ Jesus, as has been preached and taught them from the Word of God. (II:201a).

This is the very least of all the commandments which He has given. It is a much greater commandment to love your enemies, to do good to those who do evil to you, to pray in spirit and in truth for those who persecute you, to subjugate the flesh under God's word, to tread under your feet all pride, covetousness, impurity, hate, envy and intemperance, to serve your neighbor with gold, silver, with house and possessions, with your hard labor, with counsel and deed, with life and death, nay to be free from all evil desire, unbecoming words and evil works, to love God and His righteousness, will and commandments with all your heart, and to bear the cross of the Lord Jesus Christ with a joyous heart. Can the commandment of baptism be compared with any of these? I say again, it is the least of all the commandments that were given us, for it is not more than a little outward work, namely the application of a handful of water. Now he who has obtained the most important matter, namely the inward, will nevermore say, "What can water avail me," but will readily with a thankful and obedient heart hear and fulfill the words of God. But as long as he has not the inward work, he may well say, what can water avail me! (Preface to *Foundation* of 1539).

18. *Import of Baptism*

All who by the grace of God have been translated from Adam into Christ, and been made partakers of the divine nature and are baptized of God with the Spirit and fire of heavenly love will not contend so deridingly against the Lord and say: What can water avail, but they say with trembling Saul: "Lord, what wilt thou have me to do?" and with the penitent on the day of Pentecost: "Men and brethren, what shall we do?" They will renounce their own wisdom and willingly obey the word of the Lord, for they are led by His Spirit, and through faith, with willing obedient hearts perform all things commanded them of the Lord.

But so long as their minds are not renewed, and they have not the mind of Christ, Phil. 2:5; are not washed in the inner man with clean water from the living fountain of God, Heb. 10:22, they may well say, What can water avail us? For the whole ocean would not cleanse them as long as they are earthly and carnally minded. (I:38b).

19. *Infant Baptism*

Since, then, we do not find in all Scripture a single word by which Christ has ordained the baptism of infants, or that His apostles taught and practiced it, we say and confess rightly that infant baptism is but a human invention, an opinion of men, a perversion of the ordinance of Christ. (I:29b).

To baptize before that which is required for baptism, namely faith, is found is as if one would place the cart before the horse, to sow before plowing, to build before the lumber is at hand, or to seal the letter before it is written. (II:211b).

Lastly, they appeal to Origen and Augustine and say that these assert that they have obtained infant baptism from the apostles. To this we reply and inquire whether Origen and Augustine have proved it from Scripture. If they have done so, we desire to hear it. But if not, we must hear and believe Christ and His apostles, and not Augustine and Origen. (I:37a).

Again, if the infant baptists assert that infant baptism is not forbidden and that therefore it is right, I reply that it is not expressly forbidden in the Holy Scriptures to bless, as they call it, holy water, candles, palms, goblets, and robes, to hold mass and other ceremonies, yet we say rightfully that it is wrong, first because people put their trust in these things, secondly because it is done without the commandment of God, for He has commanded us not a word thereof, and never should any commandment be observed which is not contained or implied in His holy Word, either in letter or spirit. (II:214b).

Beloved, since the ordinance of Jesus Christ is unchangeable, and it alone is acceptable to the Father; and since He has commanded that the Gospel should first be preached and, secondly, those who believe baptized, it follows that those who baptize and are baptized without being taught the holy Gospel and without faith, baptize and are baptized on their own opinion, without the doctrine and command of Jesus Christ; therefore it is an ungodly, useless and vain ceremony. For had Israel circumcised their females because it was not expressly forbidden, they would have them circumcised without the ordinance of God, for He had commanded that the males should be circumcised. It is the same in this instance. If we baptize the unconscious infants, although it is not expressly forbidden in Scripture, just as it was not forbidden to circumcise the females, we baptize without the ordinance of Jesus Christ; for He commanded that those should be baptized who hear and believe His holy Gospel. Matt. 28:19; Mark 16:16; Acts 2:38; 9:18; 10:48; 16:33. (II:196b).

I know that Luther teaches that faith is present in infants, just as in a believing, sleeping man. To this I reply, first, that if there were such a sleeping faith in little unconscious infants (which however is nothing but human sophistry), it would notwithstanding be improper to baptize such children so long as they would not verbally confess it and show the required fruits. For the holy apostles did not baptize any believers while they were asleep, as we have shown in our former writings. (II:199a).

In the third place, we answer: We have in the Scriptures record of four households that have been baptized, namely that of Cornelius, of the jailor, of Lydia and of Stephanas, Acts 10:48; 16:15, 33; I Cor. 1:16, and the Scriptures clearly show that in three of these households all were believers, namely of Cornelius, Acts 10:2, 44-47, of the jailor Acts 16:34, and that of Stephanas I Cor. 16:15. But touching the household of Lydia, the reader should know that although the Scriptures say nothing definite about it, it is not usual in Scripture, nor the custom of the world, to call a family by the wife's name as long as the husband is living. Since Luke here names the house by a woman and not a man, reason teaches us that Lydia was at that time either a widow or a virgin. And how much is to be made of the supposition that there were infants in her household, we will let the God-fearing reader judge. (I:36b).

20. Salvation of Infants

And although infants have neither faith nor baptism, think not therefore that they are lost. O no! they are saved, for they have the Lord's own promise of the kingdom of God; not indeed through any element, ceremony or external rites, but only by grace through Jesus Christ. And therefore we do truly believe that grace is extended to them, yea that they are acceptable to God, pure and holy, heirs of God and of eternal life. On the ground of this promise all Christian believers may be assured of and rejoice in the truth that their children are saved. (I:36a).

If they die before they come to years of understanding and before they may hear and believe, they die under the promise of God and are saved, and this by no other means than the precious promise of grace, given through Jesus Christ, Luke 18:16. But if, having reached the years of understanding, they hear and believe, they should then be baptized. If they do not accept or believe the word when they have arrived at such age, whether they are baptized or not, they will be lost, as Christ Himself teaches, Mark 16:16. (II:198b).

For, if the children under the Old Dispensation were received into the covenant of God by circumcision and those of the New Dispensation by baptism, as he [Gellius] says, it would undeniably follow that the infants who died before the eighth day and those who were not circumcised in the wilderness [Josh. 5:5], as well as all the females, were not in the Israelitish church or congregation, and consequently had no share in the grace, covenant or promise. The same would also apply to the children who have died before they could have been baptized. O great abomination! (II:47b).

21. *The Error of Baptismal Regeneration*

To teach and believe that regeneration is obtained through baptism, my brethren, is terrible idolatry and blasphemy against the blood of Christ. For there is neither in heaven nor on earth any other remedy for our sins, be they evil propensities or transgressions, than the blood of Christ alone, as we have often shown in our first writings (I Pet. 1:19; I John 1:7; Col. 1:20). If then we ascribe remission of sin to baptism and not to the blood of Christ, we make of baptism a golden calf and place it in Christ's stead. For if we could be washed or cleansed by baptism, then Christ and His merits would be displaced, except we confess that there are two means for the remission of our sins, namely baptism and the blood of Christ. But this is not the case, nor will be in eternity, for the immaculate, most precious blood of our Lord Jesus Christ shall and must have the glory, as all prophets and apostles have so clearly prophesied and testified throughout the Scriptures. (II:200b).

22. *The Lord's Supper*

In like manner we believe and confess concerning the Lord's holy Supper, that it is a holy sacramental sign, instituted of the Lord Himself, with bread and wine, and enjoined upon His own in remembrance of Him, taught and administered also according to the institution of the Lord, by the apostles among the brethren. (II:270a).

We teach, seek, and desire that supper which Christ Jesus Himself has instituted and administered, to be observed in a church which is outwardly without spot or blemish, that is, without any known transgression and wickedness; for the church judges that of which it has knowledge but inward wickedness which is not apparent to the Church such as the betraying of Judas, of that God is to judge, for He alone tries the hearts and reins, and not the church. It is to be observed in both kinds, namely bread and wine, to the remembrance of the Lord's death and as a renewal and evidence of brotherly love. (II: 243b).

In the fifth place we teach, seek and demand that the Lord's Supper be observed as the Lord Jesus Himself has instituted and observed it, namely with a church that is outwardly without spot or blemish, that is without noticeable transgression and wickedness; for the church judges that which is visible. But what is inwardly evil, but does not appear outwardly to the church, as for example the betrayal of Judas, such God alone will judge and pass sentence on them; for He alone, and not the church, discerns hearts and reins. (II:243a).

23. *Discipline*

It is evident that a congregation or church can not continue in the salutary doctrine and in a blameless and pious life without the proper practice of discipline. Even as a city without a wall and gates, or a field without an inclosure or fence, or a house without walls and doors, so is also a church without the true apostolic exclusion or ban. For it would be open to all deceiving spirits, all godless scorners and haughty despisers, all idolatrous and insolent transgressors, yes to all lewd debauchers and adulterers, as is the case with all the great sects of the world which style themselves, although improperly, churches of Christ. In my opinion it is a leading characteristic, an honor and a means of prosperity for a true church to teach with Christian discretion the true apostolic exclusion and to observe it carefully with vigilant love according to the teaching of the holy divine Scriptures. (I:241b).

For so long as the pastors and teachers [in the primitive Christian church] earnestly taught and required a pious, godly life, served baptism and the Supper to the godly alone, and rightly practiced discipline according to the Scriptures, they were the church and congregation of Christ. (II:69b).

Therefore take heed. If you see your brother sin, do not pass by him as one that is not concerned about his soul, but if his fall be not unto death, help him to arise immediately, by loving admonition and brotherly instruction, before you eat, drink, sleep or do anything else, as one who ardently seeks his salvation, lest your poor erring brother be hardened in his sin, and perish. (II:445a).

24. *Repentance in Case of Secret Sin*

Should it at any time come to pass that any one sin against his God in secret in any carnal abomination, from which may He through His power preserve us all, and should the Spirit of the grace of Christ who alone must awaken true repentance in us all, again touch his heart and grant him genuine repentance, of this we have not to judge, for it is a matter between him and God. For since it is evident that we do not seek our righteousness and salvation, the remission of our sins, satisfaction, reconciliation and eternal life in discipline or through excommunication, but alone in the righteousness, intercession, merit, death and blood of Christ, and since now the two real objects why the ban is commanded in the Scriptures can not be sought in the instance of such an one, because, firstly, his sin is private, hence no offence can follow from it, and secondly, he is contrite at heart and penitent in life and therefore there is no need of putting him to shame in order that he may be brought to repentance, hence there is no commission of Christ, no divine command that he should be more severely taken to account, nor excluded or brought to shame before the church. (I:350).

25. The Missionary Calling of the Church

In the second place, we seek and desire with yearning ardent hearts, yea at the cost of our life and blood, that the holy Gospel of Jesus Christ and His apostles, which alone is the true doctrine and will remain until Jesus Christ will reappear in the clouds, may be taught and preached throughout all the world, as the Lord Jesus Christ commanded His disciples in the last words which He addressed to them on earth, Matt. 28:19; Mark 16:15. (II:243).

I seek and desire from my heart nothing (this He knows who knows all things) that the glorious name, the divine will and the praise of our Lord Jesus Christ may be made known throughout the world. (II:249a).

To this end we preach as much as opportunity and possibility affords, both in daytime and by night, in houses and in fields, in forests and wildernesses, in this land and abroad, in prison and bonds, in water, fire and the scaffold, on the gallows, and upon the wheel, before lords and princes, orally and by writing at the risk of possessions and life, as we have done these many years without ceasing. (II:10).

We seek and desire only that we might point the whole world (which lieth in wickedness) to the true way, and that many souls may by the Word of the Lord, through His help and power, be won from the dominion of Satan and brought to Christ. (II:302).

I strive after nothing but that the God of heaven and earth, through His blessed Son Jesus Christ may have the glory through His blessed word; that all men may be saved, and that they may awaken in this acceptable time of grace from their deep sleep of sin. (II:328).

We seek from our whole heart nothing but that we may effect the salvation of all mankind, and this not only by giving our possessions and labor, but also (understand it in an evangelical sense) our life and blood. (II:255).

This is my only joy and the desire of my heart, that I may extend the borders of the kingdom of God, make known the truth, reprove sin, teach righteousness, feed the hungry souls with the Word of the Lord, lead the stray sheep into the right path, and win many souls for the Lord through His Spirit, power and grace. (I:75).

26. *Nonresistance*

The regenerated do not go to war nor fight. They are the children of peace who have beaten their swords into plowshares and their spears into pruning hooks and know of no war. They give to Caesar the things that are Caesar's and to God the things that are God's. Their sword is the word of the Spirit which they wield with a good conscience through the Holy Ghost. (I:170b).

Since we are to be conformed to the image of Christ (Rom. 8:29), how can we, then, fight our enemies with the sword? Does not the apostle Peter say: "For even hereunto were ye called, because Christ also suffered for us, leaving us an example, that ye should follow his steps; who did no sin neither was guile found in his mouth; who, when he was reviled, reviled not again; when he suffered he threatened not; but committed himself to him that judgeth righteously" (I Pet. 2:21-23; Matt. 16:24). And this accords with the words of John who says: "He that saith he abideth in him ought himself also so to walk, even as he walked" (I John 2:6). And Christ Himself says: "Whosoever will come after me, let him deny himself, and take up his cross and follow me" (Mark 8:34; Luke 9:23). Again: "My sheep hear my voice . . . and they follow me" (John 10:27). (II:435b).

My dear reader, if the poor, ignorant world with an honest heart accepted this our hated and despised doctrine, which is not of us but of Christ, and faithfully obeyed it, they could well change their deadly swords into plowshares and their spears into pruning hooks, level their gates and walls, dismiss their executioners and henchmen. For all who accept our doctrine in its power, will by God's grace not have any ill will to any one upon earth, and not against their most bitter enemies, much less wrong and harm them by deeds and actions; for they are children of the Most High who from their hearts love that which is good and in their weakness avoid that which is evil; nay, hate it and are inimical thereto. (II:103a).

O man! man! look upon the irrational creatures and learn wisdom. All roaring lions, all frightful bears, all devouring wolves, live in peace among themselves with their own species. But you, poor, helpless creatures, created in God's own image and called rational beings, are born without teeth, claws, and horns and with a feeble nature, speechless and strengthless, yea neither able to walk nor stand, but have to depend entirely upon maternal care — to teach you that you should be men of peace and not of strife. (I:76a).

Peter was commanded to put his sword into the sheath. All Christians are bidden to love their enemies, do good to those who do them evil, and pray for those who abuse and persecute them; to give the cloak also if any one sue them at law for the coat; if they are stricken on the right cheek to turn to him who abuses them the other also. Say, beloved, how can a Christian, according to the Scriptures, consistently retaliate, rebel, war, murder, slay, torture, steal, rob and burn cities and conquer countries? Matt. 26:52; John 18:10; Matt. 5:12, 39, 40. (II:306b).

I am well aware that the tyrants who boast themselves Christians attempt to justify their horrible wars and shedding of blood, and would make a good work of it, by referring us to Moses, Joshua, etc. But they do not reflect that Moses and his successors, with their iron sword, have served out their time, and that Jesus Christ has now given us a new commandment and has girded our loins with another sword. — They do not consider that they use the sword of war, which they wield, contrary to all evangelical Scripture, against their own brethren, namely those of like faith with them who have received the same baptism and have broken the same bread with them and are thus members of the same body. (I:198).

Again, our fortress is Christ, our defence is patience, our sword is the Word of God, and our victory is the sincere, firm, unfeigned faith in Jesus Christ. Spears and swords of iron we leave to those who, alas, consider human blood and swine's blood of well nigh equal value. He that is wise, let him judge what I mean. (I:81b).

Captains, knights, soldiers and such like bloody men are offering to sell soul and body for money, and swear with uplifted hand that they will destroy cities and countries, apprehend and kill the citizens and inhabitants and rob them of their possessions, although they have never harmed them nor given them any provocation. O what an accursed, wicked, abominable business! And yet it is said that they protect the country and people and assist in administering justice! (I:137a).

27. *Swearing of Oaths*

Christ says, "Ye have heard that it has been said to them of old time: Thou shalt not forswear thyself, but shalt perform unto the Lord thine oaths. But I say unto you: Swear not at all, neither by heaven, for it is God's throne, nor by the earth, for it is his footstool," etc. (Matt. 5:33-35). And you, Micron, say that none but light-minded and false oaths are thereby prohibited, as if Moses had permitted Israel to swear light-mindedly and falsely and that to us under the New Testament only, Christ has forbidden it.

If we have the same liberty as the Israelites in this matter, as you assert . . . then tell me, why did the Lord not say: Ye have heard that it has been said to them of old time: Thou shalt not forswear thyself, and I say unto you: Obey this injunction. But he says: Moses has permitted you to swear rightly; but I say unto you: Swear not at all. (II:409a).

The oath is required for no other purpose than to obtain truthful statement and testimony. Can, then, the truth not be told without an oath? Do all tell the truth who are under oath? You will admit that the first question is to be answered in the affirmative and the second in the negative.

Is, then, the oath itself the truth of the testimony, or does the truth depend upon him who swears the oath? Why then do not the authorities require the truth to be told with yea and nay, as ordained of God, rather than with an oath which God has forbidden? For they can notwithstanding punish those who are found false in their yea and nay, the same as those who commit perjury. (II:410a).

That yea is yea and nay nay with all true Christians, is fully proved by those who, in our Netherlands, are so tyrannically visited with imprisonment, confiscation and torture, with fire, the stake and the sword, when indeed with one word they could escape all this, if they would misuse their yea and nay. But as they are born of the truth, therefore they walk in the truth, and testify to the truth unto death, as may be abundantly seen in Flanders, Brabant, Holland, West Friesland, etc. (274b).

28. *Capital Punishment*

If a criminal would truly repent before his God and be born from above, he would then be a saint and a child of God, a fellow partaker of grace, a spiritual member of the Lord's body, sprinkled with His precious blood and anointed with the Holy Spirit — and for such an one to be hanged on the gallows, executed on the wheel, burned at the stake or in any manner be harmed by another Christian who in Christ Jesus is one heart and soul with him, this I should think strange and out of place, considering the compassionate, merciful, loving disposition, spirit and example of Christ, the meek Lamb, which example He has commanded all his chosen children to follow.

Again, if he remain impenitent and his life be taken, this would be nothing else but to unmercifully cut short his time for repentance of which, in case his life were spared, he might yet avail himself; to tyrannically deliver his soul which was purchased with such a precious treasure unto the devil — never taking into consideration that the Son of Man who says, "Learn of me" (Matt. 11:28), "I have given you an example" (John 13:15), "Follow me" (Matt. 16:24), "He is not come to destroy souls, but to save them" (Matt. 18:11; Luke 19:10). (II:407b).

Profane history shows that the Lacedemonians who were heathen did not put their criminals to death but imprisoned them and put them at labor. (II:408a).

29. *Nonconformity to the World*

It would be more in accordance with evangelical requirements, if he [Gellius] would diligently point such proud and exalted persons to the humility of Christ, that they may learn to deny themselves and to consider their origin and destination, that they may repent of their excessive pomp and vanity, their superfluity and ungodliness, fear God from their hearts, walk in His ways and in true humility of heart serve their neighbors with their riches. (II:17a).

This is not a kingdom in which one adorns himself with gold, silver, pearls, silk, velvet and costly finery, as does the proud, haughty world, and also your leaders, giving you liberty to do likewise, under the excuse that it is harmless if your heart is free from it. So even Satan might excuse his pride and pretend the lust of his eye to be pure and good. But this is the kingdom of all humility in which not the outward adorning of the body but the inward adorning of the spirit is desired and sought with great zeal and diligence, with a broken heart and a contrite mind. (I:96a).

And whatsoever you do, that do in the name and fear of the Lord Jesus, and do not adorn yourself with gold, silver, pearls and embroidered hair, nor with costly, showy clothes, but dress yourselves in such apparel as becometh women of godliness and is serviceable. (I:148).

30. *Liberty of Conscience*

Tell me, kind reader, where have you, in all the days of your life read in the apostolic Scriptures, or heard, that Christ or the apostles called upon the power of the magistracy against those who would not hear their doctrine or obey their words? Yea, reader, I know to a certainty that wherever the government is to perform the ban with the sword, there is not the true knowledge, Spirit, word and church of Christ. (II:71).

Faith is a gift of God, therefore it can not be forced upon any one by worldly authorities or by the sword; alone through the pure doctrine of the holy Word and with humble ardent prayer it must be obtained of the Holy Ghost as a gift of grace. Moreover it is not the will of the Master of the house that the tares should be rooted up as long as the day of reaping is not at hand, as the Scriptural parable teaches and shows with great clearness.

Now if our persecutors are Christians, as they think, and accept the word of God, why do they not heed and follow the word and commandment of Christ? Why do they root up the tares before the time? Why do they not fear, lest they root up the good wheat, and not the tares? Why do they undertake to do the duty of angels who, at the proper time, shall bind the tares in bundles and cast them into the furnace of everlasting fire? (I:199).

Further I say: If the government rightly knew Christ and His kingdom, they would in my opinion, rather choose death, than with their worldly power and sword undertake to settle spiritual matters, which are not subject to the authority of man but to that of the great and Almighty God alone. But now they [the magistrates] are taught by their theologians that they should arrest, imprison, torture and slay those who are not obedient to their doctrine, as may, alas, be seen, in many cities and countries. (II:104).

Beloved rulers and judges, if you take to heart these cited Scriptures, and diligently reflect upon them, you will observe that your office is not your own, but God's office and service; and it is in your place to humble yourselves before His majesty, fear His great and adorable name and rightly and reasonably perform your ordained office; further that you should not so unscrupulously, with your earthly and temporal power, undertake to adjust that which belongs to the jurisdiction and kingdom of Christ, the Prince of all princes, you should not by your iron sword judge and punish that which is reserved solely for the judgment of the Most High, namely the faith and matters pertaining thereto, as also Luther and others maintained in the beginning of his labors, but after they had come to a higher and more exalted station, they have forgotten it all. (II:303).

Say, beloved, where do the Holy Scriptures teach that in Christ's kingdom and church, conscience and faith which stand under the authority of God alone, are to be regulated and ruled by the violence, tyranny, and sword of the magistracy? In what instance have Christ and the apostles ever done, advised or commanded this? For Christ says simply: "Beware of the false prophets," and Paul commands that a heretic is to be shunned after one or two admonitions. John says that we shall not greet or receive into our houses the transgressor who does not bring the doctrine of Christ. But they say not: Down with the heretics, arraign them before the magistrates, imprison them, drive them from cities and countries, cast them into the fire and water, as the Romish have done for many years, and even now is found to a great extent among you who fancy yourselves to adhere to the Word of God. (II:118).

Besides, the proud, carnal, worldly, idolatrous and tyrannical princes who do not know God (I speak of the evil princes) set up their mandates, decrees and laws as authoritative, however much they may be contradictory to God and His blessed Word; just as if the almighty Father, the Creator of all things who holds heaven and earth in His hands, who rules all things by the Word of His power, had ordained them to command, rule and according to their own judgment prescribe ordinances not only in the temporal kingdom of this perishable world, but also in the heavenly kingdom of our Lord Jesus Christ. O no, beloved, no. This is not the will of God, but it is an abomination in His sight if mortal man will usurp for himself His authority. (II:238).

I think, beloved brethren, that I have clearly shown that the excuses of the tyrants by which they would avert their tyrannical murdering to be just and right, are heathenish in principle. (I:205).

31. *Predestination*

Zwingli taught that the will of God actuated a thief to steal and a murderer to kill, and that their punishment was also brought about by the will of God — which in my opinion is an abomination above all abominations. (II: 294b).

What shall I say, dear Lord? Shall I say that Thou hast ordained the wicked to wickedness, as some have said? Be that far from me. I know, O Lord, that Thou art good and nothing evil can be found in Thee. We are the works of Thy hand, created in Christ Jesus unto good works, that we should walk therein. Life and death hast Thou left to our choice. Thou willest not the death of the sinner, but that he should repent and live. Thou art the eternal light, therefore hatest Thou all darkness; Thou desirest not that any should perish, but that all repent, come to a knowledge of Thy truth and be saved. O dear Lord, so grievously have they blasphemed Thine unspeakably great love, Thy mercy and majesty that they have made Thee, the God of all grace and Creator of all things, a very devil, saying that Thou art the cause of all evil — Thou who art called the Father of lights. Of a surety evil can not come from good, nor light from darkness, nor life from death; yet do they ascribe their stubborn hearts and carnal minds to Thy will, in order that they may continue upon the broad way and have a cover for their sins. (I: 221b).

32. *Perfectionism*

Think not, beloved reader, that we say this to boast that we be perfect and sinless. By no means.

We do not believe nor teach that we are saved by our merits and works, as our accusers falsely assert, but alone through grace by Christ Jesus, as has been said before. (II:262 seq.).

Because we teach from the mouth of the Lord: He who would enter into life, must keep the commandments (Matt. 19:17; Mark 10:19; John 15:10); in Christ neither circumcision nor uncircumcision avail but the keeping of the commandments of God (I Cor. 7:19); this is the love of God that we keep His commandments and His commandments are not grievous, I John 5:3; therefore we are called by the preachers heaven stormers and work saints, and must hear that we would be saved by our merits, although we have always confessed and shall through God's grace confess in eternity that we can not be saved by any other means in heaven or upon earth, than alone through the merits, intercession, death, and blood of Christ, as has been fully set forth above.

Behold, thus have these perverse people changed the very best to the very worst. They do not observe that all Scripture clearly condemns all wanton, haughty despisers and transgressors of God's commandments who plainly prove by their deeds that they are strangers to the saving grace of God, do not believe in Jesus Christ and according to Scripture abide in condemnation, wrath and death (John 3:36). (II:317).

But that they say we are hypocrites, and lie concerning us that we assert to be without sin, is, because we teach with all Scripture a life that shows the fruits of penitence; we testify with holy Paul that perjurers, adulterers, idolaters, drunkards, avaricious, liars, unrighteous shall not inherit the kingdom of God (I Cor. 6:10; Gal. 5:21; Eph. 5:5), that those who are carnally minded shall die, Rom. 8:13; and with John that those who sin (understand purposely or wantonly) are of the devil (I John 3:8); and therefore we have in our weakness a heartfelt dismay of such works; so often we have with Moses confessed by mouth and writing and ever will confess, that none is innocent before God, on account of the inborn nature (Gen. 6:5; 8:21), and with Isaiah that we are all as the unclean (Isa. 64:6) etc. (II:316).

33. *New Revelations*

Again, I have no visions or angelic revelations, neither do I seek or desire such, lest I be thereby deceived. For Christ's Word alone is sufficient for me. If I do not follow His testimony, then verily all is lost. And even if I had such revelations, which is not the case, they could not deviate from the Word and spirit of Christ, or else they would be only imagination, seduction and satanic deception. (II:248a).

34. *Higher Education*

Reader, do not misunderstand me. Learning and a knowledge of languages I have never in my life despised, but have from my youth honored and loved. Although I have not acquired them, yet (thanks be to God) I am not so bereft of my senses that I should despise or ridicule the knowledge of the languages through which the precious word of divine grace has come to us. I wish from my heart that I and all the pious possessed such learning, if we could in true humility use it rightly to the praise of our God and the service of our neighbor, in the pure fear of God. (II:145b).

35. *Anti-Secrecy*

Lo, kind reader, thus we have from the beginning of our ministry been ready and desirous to give an account of our faith to every person who asked it in good faith, whether they were ruler or citizen, learned or unlearned, rich or poor, man or woman. And today we are ready to do so as far as is possible to us, for we are not ashamed of the Gospel of the glory of Christ. If any one desire to hear from us, we are prepared to teach; if any one wish to know our principles, it is our hearty desire, if our writings do not suffice, to explain them clearly. — For it is our earnest endeavor that the truth may be brought to light. But the bloodthirsty murder of Antichrist must not be attempted, I say, for it is of the devil and inconsistent to a Christian. (II:321b).

36. *Attitude Toward Other Denominations*

My reader, understand me rightly. That God should not have His elect among the above named churches [the persecuting state churches], concerning this we do not dispute, but shall in humility leave this both now and forever to the gracious judgment of God; ... but the question under dispute is with what spirit, doctrine, sacraments, ordinances and life Christ has commanded to gather unto Him an abiding church and maintain it in His ways. (II:94).

37. *Examples of Consecration to the Lord's Service*

Yes, dear reader, the true Christian faith, as the Scripture requires, is so living, active and powerful with all those who through the grace of the Lord have rightly received it, that they, for the word and testimony of the Lord, do not hesitate to forsake father and mother, wife and children, money and possessions, to suffer all scorn and disgrace, hardships and dangers, and finally to have their poor weak bodies which are so fearful of suffering, burned at the stake, as may be frequently seen and observed in the instances of so very many people and faithful witnesses of Jesus, especially in these our Netherlands.

Alas! how many did I formerly know, and know the greater part of them now, both men and women, young men and maidens (would to God that they be increased, to His praise and to the salvation of all the world, to many hundred thousand) who from the inmost of their souls seek Christ and His word and lead a pious, unblamable life (yet ever in weakness) before God and all men; they are sincere and sound in doctrine, unblamable, I say, in their life, full of the fear and love of God, helpful to everyone, merciful, compassionate, humble, sober, chaste, not refractory or seditious, but quiet and peaceable, obedient to the government in all things that are not contrary to God; and yet, they have for a number of years seldom slept on their own beds and do not now. For they are hated of the world in such a measure that they are persecuted without mercy, betrayed, apprehended, exiled and robbed of their property and life, like highway men, thieves and murderers. And this for no other reason than only that they out of true fear of God, do not dare to have a part in the abominable carnal life nor the cursed shameful idolatry of this blind world. (I:158).

Inasmuch as it is found in fact and in truth that our faithful brethren and sisters in Christ Jesus, the beloved companions in the tribulation and in the kingdom and patience of Jesus Christ (Rev. 1:9), so sincerely fear and love the Lord, their God, that rather than knowingly and willfully speak a false word [denying that they were baptized] or to act hypocritically contrary to God's Word [keeping themselves against their convictions outwardly in the state church in order to shun persecution]; they would give their good name, reputation, as well as their money, goods, bodies, and everything of which human nature may be desirous, as a prey to the bloodthirsty; therefore we would leave it to the judgment of your Excellencies and Honors, whether they are such pernicious, evil people as, alas, they are called by many, and generally adjudged. (II:109).

I do not esteem my natural life to be better than the beloved men of God did their lives. I can be deprived of nothing except this perishable mortal flesh which at some time must die and return to dust (even if I should live to the age of Methuselah). A hair shall not fall from my head without the will of my heavenly Father. If I lose my life for the sake of Christ and His testimony, and on account of my sincere love to my neighbor (in whose salvation I am interested) I know of a certainty that I shall save it to life eternal. Therefore I can not keep the truth to myself, but I must testify to it and set it forth without hypocrisy in the true fear of God, to my beloved Lords. (I:78b).

38. *Laboring under Difficulties*

He who has purchased me with the blood of His love and has called me unworthily to His service, knows me and knows that I seek neither earthly possessions nor a life of ease, but only the praise of my Lord, my salvation and the salvation of many souls. For this I, my poor, feeble wife and little children have for nearly eighteen years endured extreme anxiety, oppression, affliction, homelessness and persecution and must at all times be in danger of life and great peril. Yea when the ministers of the national churches repose on easy beds and downy pillows, we generally have to hide in secluded corners. When they at weddings and baptismal dinners [held when the rite of baptism was observed] are unbecomingly entertained with pipe and tambour and lute, we must stand in apprehension when the dogs bark, that the catchpolls are at hand.

Whilst they are saluted as doctors, preachers and masters by everyone, we must hear that we are Anabaptists, hedge preachers, seducers and heretics and must be saluted in the devil's name. In short, whilst they are richly rewarded for their service with large incomes and easy times, our recompense and portion must be fire, the sword, and death.

Behold my faithful reader, in such anxiety, poverty, oppression and danger of death have I, a homeless man, to this hour constantly performed the service of my Lord, and I hope through His grace to continue therein to His glory, as long as I remain in this earthly tabernacle. What I and my faithful coworkers have sought or could have sought in these arduous and dangerous labors, is from the works and the fruits apparent to all the well-disposed.

Yea, it has come to this (may God make it better) that where four or five, ten or twenty, have met in the name of the Lord, to speak of the word of the Lord and to do His work, in whose midst Christ is, who fear God with all their heart and lead a pious, unblamable life before all the world, that if they are caught at a meeting or if accusation is brought against them, they must be delivered up to be burned at the stake, or drowned in the water. But those who met in the name of Belial . . . in public houses of ill fame and the accursed drunken taverns, who live in open disgrace and act wickedly against God's word, such live in all freedom and peace. (I:78b).

In short dear reader, if the merciful Lord had not, in His great love, tempered the hearts of some of the rulers and magistrates, but had let them proceed according to the instigations and blood-preaching of their theologians, no pious person would survive. But yet a few are found who, notwithstanding the words and writings of all theologians, tolerate the exiles and for a time show them mercy, for which we will forever give praise to God, the Most High, and also return our thanks in all love to such kind and discreet rulers. (II:104b).

When I was of the world, I spake and did as the world and the world hated me not. — While I served the world, the world rewarded me. All men spake well of me even as their fathers did of the false prophets. But now that I love the world with a godly love, seek from my heart its salvation and blessing, admonish, instruct, and rebuke it with Thy holy Word and point it to the crucified Christ Jesus, the world has become to me a grievous cross and a gall of bitterness. So great is its hatred that not only

I myself but also all who show me love, mercy and favor must in some places look for imprisonment and death. O blessed Lord, I am considered by them more unfavorable than a notorious thief and murderer. (I:225b).

39. *Persecution*

How many pious children of God have they for the testimony of God and their conscience' sake within a few years deprived of their homes and possessions, have confiscated their needed property, and committed it to the bottomless money chests of the Emperor; how many have they betrayed, driven out of cities and countries and put them to the stocks and torture, turning the poor orphans naked into the streets. Some they have hanged, some they have tortured with inhuman tyranny and afterwards choked them with cords at the stake. Some they roasted and burned alive. — Some they have killed with the sword and given them to the fowls of the air to devour. Some they have cast to the fishes; some had their houses destroyed; some have been cast into slimy bogs. Some had their feet cut off, one of whom I have seen and conversed with. Others wander about here and there, in want, homelessness and affliction in mountains and deserts, in holes and caves of the earth, as Paul says. They must flee with their wives and little children from one country to another, from one city to another. They are hated, abused, slandered and belied by all men. By the theologians and magistrates they are denounced. They are deprived of their food, are driven forth in the cold winter and pointed at with the finger of scorn; yea whoever can assist in the persecution of the poor oppressed Christians, thinks he has done God service, as Christ says, John 16:2. (I: 196a).

If a thief is led to the gallows, a murderer is broken upon the wheel, or another malefactor punished by an uncommonly painful manner of death, everyone inquires what he has done. The sentence is not pronounced as long as the judges do not fully understand the facts and know the truth concerning his evil deeds. But whenever an innocent contrite Christian whom the gracious Lord has rescued from the evil, wicked ways of sin and brought upon the way of peace, is accused by the priests and preachers and brought before their court, they do not consider him worthy to really investigate what reasons and Scripture move him that he will no longer listen to the priests and preachers . . . they do not desire to know why he has mended his life and received the baptism of Christ, or what may be his motive that he is willing to suffer and die for his faith. They only ask whether he is baptized. If the answer is in the affirmative the sentence is fixed and he must die. (I:149b).

Since it is manifest that the whole world is so inimically embittered against us, although undeservedly, that we are not suffered to be heard or seen, and many an innocent sheep of the Lord, many a God-fearing one who is not a teacher is led to the slaughter here and there, is without all mercy executed and murdered with the sword, water and fire, and that to us homeless teachers not anywhere under the heavens is given so much as a pigsty to live in liberty with the knowledge and consent of the authorities, but through public mandates we are judged before we are apprehended and condemned before we are convicted, and since such conditions did to my knowledge nowhere prevail in the times of the apostles, therefore I pray all my readers for God's sake to consider in the fear of the Lord what great injustice Gellius and his friends have done us, through his perverted, bitter words, viz., night-preaching, hedge-preaching, etc., when we can not do otherwise, as is well known. . . . We are prepared at all times to render an account of our faith to everyone, and to defend the truth, whenever it can be done in good faith without deceit and secret intent at our lives. (II:11-13).

The said doctrine of the holy divine Word we have had in the German countries for many years, and have it daily more and more in such power and clearness that it is palpable and evident that it is the finger and work of God. For the haughty become humble, the avaricious liberal, the drunkards sober, the unchaste pure, etc. For the word of God is accepted of them with such assurance that they do not hesitate to forsake father and mother, husband, wife and children, their possessions and life on account of it, and willingly suffer death. For many are burned at the stake, many drowned, many executed with the sword, many imprisoned, exiled and their property confiscated. Nevertheless all avails nothing with the obdurate persecutors. If it is only said, when a poor innocent one of the sheepfold of the Lord has been slaughtered, "He is an Anabaptist," it is believed sufficient. They do not require what proof and scriptural grounds he had, of what nature his conduct and life was, whether he injured any one or not. Neither do they reflect or consider that it must be a special work and power . . . to cause a man to suffer unspeakable infamy and shame, great persecution and misery and often death, as you may see.

However lamentably we may here be persecuted, oppressed, smitten, robbed, burned at the stake, drowned in the water by the hellish Pharoah and his cruel, unmerciful servants, yet soon shall come the day of our refreshing and all the tears shall be wiped from our eyes and we shall be arrayed in the white silken robes of righteousness, follow the Lamb, and with Abraham, Isaac and Jacob sit down in the kingdom of God and possess the precious, pleasant land of eternal, imperishable joy. Praise God and lift up your heads, ye who suffer for Jesus' sake; the time is near when ye shall hear, "Come ye blessed" and ye shall rejoice with Him for evermore. (I: 122b).

40. *A Prayer of Menno Simons*

O Lord, I am assured that neither life nor death, neither angels nor principalities, nor powers, neither things present nor things to come, neither height nor depth nor any other creature shall separate us from Thy love which is in Christ Jesus. Yet, I know not myself; all my trust is in Thee. Though I have drunk a little of the cup of Thy suffering, yet I have not tasted it to the bottom. For when dungeon and bonds are suffered, when death by water, fire and sword are threatened, then will the gold be separated from the wood, the silver from straw, the pearls from stubble. Then do not forsake me, gracious Lord; for I know that trees of deepest root may be torn up from the earth by the violence of the storm, and the lofty, firm mountains are rent asunder by the force of the earthquake. Have not Job and Jeremiah, the true examples of endurance, stumbled in Thy way through weakness of the flesh? Therefore I pray Thee, blessed Lord, according to Thy faithfulness and grace, suffer me not to be tempted above that I am able to bear, lest my soul be made ashamed in eternity. I pray not for my flesh; I well know that it is subject to suffering and death. For this alone I pray, forsake me not in the time of trial but make a way of escape in my hour of temptation; deliver me of all my need, for I put my trust in Thee. (Meditation to the Twenty-fifth Psalm, 1539, fol. D1).

O Lord, O dear Lord, grant to Thy poor little flock that it may not be entirely swallowed up by the wrathful dragon, but that we by Thy grace may through patience overcome through the sword of Thy mouth, and may leave an ever abiding seed which shall keep Thy commandments, preserve Thy testimony and forever praise Thy great and glorious name. Amen, dear Lord, Amen. (83a).

CHRONOLOGICAL LIST OF MENNO SIMONS' WRITINGS

PLAIN AND CLEAR PROOF AGAINST THE BLASPHEMY OF JOHN OF LEIDEN
THE SPIRITUAL RESURRECTION
MEDITATION ON THE TWENTY-FIFTH PSALM
THE NEW BIRTH
THE FOUNDATION
CHRISTIAN BAPTISM
THE REASON WHY I DO NOT CEASE TEACHING
OF THE TRUE CHRISTIAN FAITH
LOVING ADMONITION, ON DISCIPLINE
BRIEF AND CLEAR CONFESSION, TO JOHN A' LASCO
CLEAR ACCOUNT ON EXCOMMUNICATION
CONFESSION OF THE TRIUNE GOD
QUESTIONS AND ANSWERS, ON DISCIPLINE
CONFESSION CONCERNING JUSTIFICATION, ETC.
BRIEF DEFENSE TO ALL THEOLOGIANS
HUMBLE SUPPLICATION TO ALL MAGISTRATES
DEFENSE AND REPLY CONCERNING FALSE ACCUSATIONS
THE CROSS OF CHRIST
REPLY TO GELLIUS FABER
CONFESSION, ON THE INCARNATION OF CHRIST (REPLY TO A' LASCO)
REPLY TO MARTIN MICRON
DUTIES TOWARD CHILDREN
INSTRUCTION ON THE EXCOMMUNICATION
ANSWER TO ZYLIS AND LEMKE

www.ingramcontent.com/pod-product-compliance
Lightning Source LLC
Chambersburg PA
CBHW070921180426
43192CB00038B/2105